Unlocking
The Secrets
Of
Successful Women
In Business

**Linda Brakeall
Anna Wildermuth**

What real people are saying about this book:

Charm and Charisma are like illusive Genies who escaped from a bottle. The authors captured the essence of the two. They remind you of the subtle lessons mothers are forgetting to teach their daughters in this day and age such as how to dress and what to say to radiate your own natural charm and charisma. Well done ladies!

– Carol Johnson
Vice President, Business Development e-neightbors.com

This book addresses very real and practical topics necessary to enhance the success potential for businesswomen. I've trained my sales people and others, and still I found good, new hints on selling in this book. As a new professional speaker, I found useful new ideas in <u>Unlocking The Secrets</u>. I particularly enjoyed the how-to-approach. . . . a stimulating reference for any professional woman wanting to augment her business career possibilities.

—Linda McCabe, owner Feminine Forum, former owner of H. Diamond Iron & Metal Co., founded in 1919.

It's clear Linda and Anna know the rules of the game when it comes to women in the business world. Their humor and straightforward advice will help many to understand how to become more successful.

– Ellen Schnur
Event Producer

As an employer of women, I found many insights into how women think, "process" information and how they react. This book is helping me to more effectively utilize their skills and talents.

– Mark Boersma, Owner
Synergy Solutions

You can achieve personal and professional success through this holistic approach. This is the first book of its kind that addresses all the areas that women need to know about in order to succeed in business.

– M. J. Takagi
Livingston County Homebuilders Association

(The information in this book) …really gave me an edge when I worked with the media while I was campaigning for the Illinois State Legislature. … invaluable in our last two successful campaigns, and I highly recommend it!

—Suzanne Bassi
Illinois State Legislature.

"…informative, knowledgeable and as quick and easy to read as A,B,C. An excellent resource for any businesswoman.

— Judi Edenson
Author of <u>Lily's Garden.</u>

I am 28 years old and work in a law office as the Director of Client Relations. I found this book offered me all the information I need in order to get people to take me seriously as professional. Not only the tips on dressing and speaking better, but the information on how we, as women, are perceived in the business world. This book has really opened my eyes!

– Amy Mulkey
Director of Client Relations

As a reporter, I covered an "Unlocking the Secrets," seminar and I not only got a great story, but a lot of ideas for me personally. I am setting goals and seeing them come true after only a week. I pay more attention to what my outward look is saying about who I am.

– John E. Aho
Staff Writer, Insider Business Journal

Unlocking The Secrets Of Successful Women In Business

**Linda Brakeall
Anna Wildermuth**

HAWTHORNE PRESS
BOOKS FOR PROFESSIONAL WOMEN

Unlocking The Secrets
Of Successful Women In Business
By Linda Brakeall and Anna Wildermuth

Hawthorne Press
11 Arrow Wood, Suite 2D
Hawthorn Woods, IL 60047
orders@unlockingthesecrets.com

All rights reserved. No part of this book may be reproduced or transmitted in any form or by any means, electronic or mechanical, including photocopying, recording or by any information storage or retrieval system, without written permission from the authors, except for the inclusion of brief quotations in a review. No liability is assumed for use of the information within.
© 2001 By Linda Brakeall And Anna Wildermuth

"Unlocking The Secrets" is a trademark of Hawthorne Press.

Manufactured in the United States of America.

Library of Congress Cataloging-in-Publication Data

Brakeall, Linda
Unlocking the secrets of successful women in business /
Linda Brakeall, Anna Wildermuth.
--Hawthorn Woods, IL:
Hawthorne Press, 2001
p.cm. (Unlock the secrets)

IBSN 0-9710209-0-6 (pbk)
1. Success in business -- Handbooks, manuals, etc.
2. Businesswomen -- Handbooks, manuals, etc.
I. Wildermuth, Anna
II. Title.
III. Series.

HF5386.B73 2001   2001- 089365
650.1/082--dc21   CIP

This book is dedicated to all the women who want to get into the game, but never had a rulebook . . . before now.

**Our Sincere Appreciation
to Mark Victor Hansen
Who Gave Us The Courage To Proceed!**

Ten percent of all profits from the sale of <u>Unlocking the Secrets of Successful Women in Business</u> will be donated to WINGS. (Women In Need Growing Stronger.) WINGS is a not-for-profit comprehensive housing program dedicated to ending homelessness for women and children in the northwest suburbs of Chicago. It is the mission of the WINGS program to provide a personal growth program in a transitional living setting for homeless suburban women and their children. WINGS help them learn to manage their lives through education, guidance and support. The women live in apartments and multiple family homes in residential neighborhoods while going to school, working and caring for themselves and their children. The ultimate goal of WINGS is to help these women become self-sufficient and they succeed far more often than any other program with which we are familiar!

If you'd like more information about this amazing organization, visit their web site at www.wingsprogram.com.

Invest in the human soul.
Who knows, it might be a diamond in the rough.
Mary McLeod Bethune

It appears to me impossible that I should cease to exist,
or that this active, restless spirit, equally alive to joy
and sorrow, should be only organized dust —
ready to fly abroad the moment the spring snaps,
or the spark goes out, which kept it together.
Surely something resides in this heart that is not
perishable -- and life is more than a dream.
Mary Wollstonecraft

Table Of Contents

Introduction — 15

Key 1 Where Are You Now? — 25
    Is Your Appearance Up To Date?
    Is It Quick And Easy To Look Smart?
    How Do You Feel About Your Body?
    How Are You Perceived When You Speak And Sell?
    Do You Know The Rules Of Business Etiquette And Communication?
    Discovery Exercises

Key 2 It's Not Easy Being A Successful Woman In Business! — 34
    What Is A Woman To Do?
    "How Do I Get Them To Take Me Seriously?"
    It's Not Always A Case Of Women Being Discriminated Against

Key 3 Getting To The Top — 41
    The Stats
    What's Wrong With This Picture?
    Why Are We Co-Conspirators?

Helping Business Women Bridge The Gender Communication Gap
By Guest Columnist Rosalind Sedacca

Sometimes We Shoot Ourselves In The Foot Because We Don't Know How To Fight Or Disagree Without Being Disagreeable

How Do You Deal With Conflict?
By Guest Columnist Carter Johnson

Sometimes We Shoot Ourselves In The Foot Because We Want People To Like Us

Key 4   Charm And Charisma In Business, In Sales, In Speaking And In Person!   58

Charming And Charismatic Women Are Comfortable With Their Bodies When They Speak!

The Art Of Small Talk!

Charming Charismatic Women Are Likeable and FUN!

Charismatic Women Have Fun When They Lose Their Train Of Thought!

Projecting Your Charm and Charisma In Sales and Interviews

Key 5   Personal Style!   85

Discover, Develop and Define Your Own Personal Style

Key 6   Professional Style   93

Your Professional Style Starts With Personal Style

No Need To Follow All Rules All The Time!

4 Keys To Successful Professional Style

Key 7   Business Casual   **107**

   Does Biz-Caz Affect Productivity?

   Business Casual Rules for Women Executives and Will-Be Executives

   Business Casual: Is Your Company Losing Money?
   By Guest Columnist Dawn E. Waldrop

Key 8   Approachability!   **110**

   Color, Ethnicity and Diversity

   5 Keys To Being Approachable

Key 9   Color Codes   **116**

   Industry Color Codes

   The Psychology And Symbolic Language Of Color

   The Energy Of Color And Fashion Feng Shui
   By Guest Columnist Denise Butchko

Key 10 What Do You Wear. . .?   **127**

   Sales Calls and Job Interviews

   Important Meeting With Boss, Peers, Or Co-Workers

   Asking For A Raise or a Promotion

   A Stressful Meeting Or Presentation

   Professional Attire For A Business Casual
      Conference Off - Site

   Dinner Parties

   "Black Tie" Business Event

   Television Interview

   Radio Interview

   Running For Political Office

Tips for Debates And Official Public Appearances

Corporate or Charity Board

5 Keys To Wearing The "Right Thing"

Key 11   Business Travel And Packing   144

Key 12   Buy The Right Professional Clothes   150

Learn What Quality Looks and Feels Like

Does The Suit Suit You? Courtesy Of E-How.com

Check Fabric And Stitching Before You Buy
Courtesy Of E-How.com

Tailored Business Basics

You ask, "How Much Should I Pay For My Clothes?"

Savvy Shopping For A Professional Wardrobe

Key 13   Maintaining Your Professional Image   170

5 Keys To Maintaining A Professional Wardrobe

Key 14   The Shapes Of Goddesses!   176

Six Basic Figure Shapes

Determining Your Shape

Key 15   Working With Your Shape   189

Seven Keys To Shape-Flattering

Appearing Taller And Slimmer

If You Are Really Tall And Thin Or If You Want To Look Heavier

Key Areas For A Perfect Fit

Key 16   Business Makeup, Hair And Grooming   202

Key 17   Business Etiquette/Professional Grace   212

   Professional Grace
      Remembering Names
      The Professional Handshake
      Personal Space

   Business Etiquette 2001 Or Traditional Etiquette?
   By Guest Columnist Gloria Peterson

   Introduction Etiquette

   Dining Etiquette
      Dining Embarrassments
      Hosting A Business Meal

Key 18   Business Communication Etiquette   226

   Professional Voice Mail

   Professional Correspondence

   Professional Success In Cyberspace

Key 19   Interviewing For A New Job   234

   Prepare To Fit In

   Do Your Homework!

   Make Your Outside Match Your Inside!

   The Rules For Getting A Job Are Just Like The Rules For Dating

Key 20   Verbal Power   247

Key 21   Why Don't Salespeople, Job Seekers, Or Speakers Have Prepared Presentations?   254

Key 22 Sales Presentation Homework   262

Key 23 Preparing Your Sales Presentation   276

Key 24 Landing The Sale!   299

Key 25 Presenting To Big And Small Clients 304
   Your Basic Preparation
   Customize Every Presentation

Key 26 Deliver A Formal Speech   310
   - Speech Dynamics
   - Microphones 101
   - Show Time!

   Epigraph   324

   Resources   328

Unlocking The Secrets of Successful Women in Business

Introduction

Have You Ever Felt That You...

🗝 Just didn't "look right?"

🗝 Ought to be the one making the speech, but didn't know how??

🗝 Needed some sales skills?

🗝 Didn't understand all the rules of business etiquette?

🗝 Were self-conscious and charm-free?

Do You Think Those Things Affect A Career?

If you wanted to improve in some or all of those areas, where would you find the guidance you need? If you had lots of time, you could read a book or more on each topic. You could spend hours (or days!) on the Internet sifting through thousands of websites. *Or ... Your worries could be over right now!*

We offer you rules, suggestions, perspective and practical tips on how to dress, speak, conduct yourself and sell, with charm, charisma, power, polish and panache! In this book you'll find the keys to unlock your success!

Unlock The Secrets Of Charm And Charisma!

It's sometimes difficult to feel charming, comfortable and confident when youre in a new situation or meeting an intimidating client. We'll teach you how to make friends fast and easily.

Unlock The Secrets Of Your Very Own Visual Style

They say you never have a second chance to make a first impression and we all know that first impressions last. Make sure they see the *authentic professional you* the first time and power-boost yourself to the next level of success!

Unlock The Secrets And Rules Of Business Etiquette

Understanding the rules for introductions, dining, entertaining and communication help you become comfortable and gracious while putting others at ease.

Unlock The Secrets Of Speaking And Selling Effectively

Those who can speak and sell have a distinct advantage in the business world because those two things form the basis of all communication.

> I do not wish women to have power over men;
> but over themselves.
> Mary Wollstonecraft

Unlocking The Secrets of Successful Women in Business

Why Did We Write This Book?

The authors share a mission to help you match your inside to your outside; both visually and verbally. Simplicity and consistency of image and message are the keys to success.

Following that mission, this book is organized very simply. Read what you need!

- 🔑 If you like tests, take the short tests.
- 🔑 If you like to analyze, do the "discovery exercises"
- 🔑 On the last page of each chapter, you will find a built-in workbook for you to record your notes, insights, inspirations and action steps.

The Authors

Anna Wildermuth, owner of Personal Images Inc., is a certified professional image strategist. She is one of those people who understands the power of clothes and loves to see people bloom when they feel confident about themselves. She recognizes quality, line and design, and instinctively knows what "works." She understands that the "uniform" created for an attorney, a Fortune 500 VP, and a professional in the health care field may all have some elements in common but there are decided differences, which enhance or diminish your credibility.

Anna has been recognized as an image expert since 1983. She has helped executives and management teams of many large corporations strategize their professional image and she understands the nuances of business and social etiquette and diversity.

Anna is a tall, slim, dramatic, restrained Asian woman who is a clothes-horse and loves fashion, shopping, and movies. Anna is the primary author of the visual and business etiquette sections.

Linda Brakeall and Anna Wildermuth

From Anna:

As a young, first generation Asian American, I remember longing to be accepted socially in a wealthy non-Asian school. For my 13th birthday, my dad took me shopping and we purchased a gray, pleated skirt with inserts of red and navy because it was the "in thing" to wear. For that same birthday, my godmother gave me an orange, red and yellow flowered blouse. I wore them together, thinking I looked "cool" because they were so much better than the ruffled dresses my mother had always made for me! I wore this "ensemble" daily for a week before my godmother found the courage to tell me you don't mix prints and plaids together; especially this, shall we say, "vivid" combination!

Although I was an honor student and involved in many activities, it seemed apparent that I was "right off the boat!" It makes a great funny story now, and almost 30 years later in certain settings, and certain situations, that very outfit might be considered "fashion forward" or daring. But it didn't work then, and I didn't know any better! How many times have you walked into a room and just knew you didn't fit in but weren't exactly sure why?

Speaking from my own experience, it's never too late or too early to begin the ongoing process of developing an authentic visual image. As I look back on my late teens, I realize that I fit in better academically than socially. Although my neighborhood was very affluent, my family had little money. My parents were first generation Chinese and we lived behind the family business. Socially, I was exposed to highly intelligent people, wonderful houses, and fine dining. It was different at home.

During those years, I desperately wanted to look "like they did." I wanted to belong, I wanted to look smart and affluent like my friends so I tried to replicate their look.

Unlocking The Secrets of Successful Women in Business

That happens in business today when people try to copy others. My advice, "Be yourself. Observe, read, and learn all you can and develop your own style." Your very own style is a combination of what you like, what works well for you, your coloring, and your shape.

Then consider what adjustments you need to make to reflect your profession. You will continue making adjustments... probably forever!

Your visual image needs to be tied to who you are. The bigger picture of style expresses your internal values and lifestyle through your external image.

As you grow and mature, personally and professionally you'll discover what to do, say and wear to help you feel confident wherever you are and whatever you do. You'll find your own attractive style, and in this case "attractive" means not only lovely, but also magnetic. You'll be able to draw people to you, you'll be comfortable with who you are and that is the most attractive aspect of anyone.

If you ever want to discuss your image, your company's image with me, or are interested in workshops, seminars or coaching, e-mail me at Anna@personalimagesinc.com.

All the best to you! **Anna**

Linda Brakeall, President of Phoenix Seminars, and long time active member of the National Speakers Association, has been speaking with microphone in hand since age 14. Her wide-ranging background includes teaching, selling, writing, managing, training and speaking. Linda left corporate America as a vice president in 1992 to become a professional speaker.

She speaks and trains in several industries, offering penetrating insights and validation to sales teams and management. Linda has had over 400 magazine articles published dealing with sales, marketing, communication and management issues over the last eight years and hosted a cable TV show interviewing Chicago business leaders.

Linda's goal for every speech, seminar and consultation is to help people make simple but profound life and work changes that positively impact their immediate environment and, in turn, the world. People who work with Linda Brakeall find that they've gained not only the tools for success, but also the willingness to take action.

Linda is a shorter, curvier, outspoken redhead who would rather "wrassle alligators" than shop for anything! Linda is the primary author of the verbal, sales, charisma, management, and presentation sections.

From Linda:
Most people rank their biggest fears in this order: cancer, public speaking and death. Now isn't that weird? For those of you who are "deathly" afraid of public speaking, you're probably shaking your head and muttering,

> **"No, that's not weird. I <u>would</u> rather die than speak in public. I'd probably lose my lunch if I stood up and had to speak in front of a room full of people." And perhaps you think, "Yeah, and at least when you <u>die</u>, they don't laugh at you!"**

Intellectually, I empathize with you, but I've had very little first hand knowledge of anything more than mild nerves. For years I didn't "get it."

One day an old friend, Audrey Beauvais, explained it to me. We were discussing this very thing and I said, "I just don't get it! What's so hard about telling a bunch of people the very same thing you'd tell one or two people?"

Unlocking The Secrets of Successful Women in Business

She said: "When was the very first time that most people had to get up and 'speak' to a room full of people?" (She didn't ask about me, 'cause I've been doing that since I was 14!) I didn't know the answer, so she prompted me, "When they took speech 101, in high school or college."

Still dim, I replied, "And..."

"And," she said, "What does anyone know at that age? What do you have to talk about? You're young and dumb and self-conscious! Most of the teachers who taught speech 101 – at least until recently – had never spoken anywhere other than a classroom! They tended to offer lame suggestions on what to talk about and they were often more critical than kind about a performance!"

I was starting to tune in, but it was still fuzzy as Audrey continued, "So a 17 or 18 year old kid was embarrassed to tears in front of a room full of his or her peers and vowed never to feel that way again!"

Eureka! I got it! Audrey was telling me that most folks who are afraid of public speaking are still listening to that embarrassed 17 or 18 year old! Ten, twenty or thirty years later! I do believe she's right! We all know that sort of thing is true in other areas, but until Audrey explained it to me, I had never applied it to this situation.

You will get better by simply speaking more often!
Here are a few places you can get some practice:

🔑 Join Toastmasters, an organization devoted to helping people develop speaking skills. Call their national office at 949-858-8255 or check their website: toastmasters.org to find a club near you.

🔑 Become president of a community or civic organization and speak at meetings.

🔑 Speak or a do training sessions at your own company.

Presenting well is one of those skills that some folks take for granted and most folks dread. This book will get your skills up to speed, then you can put on your Nikes and *just do it!* You can learn this. Let me help.

As a reader of this book, please consider me a mentor and that means that you can e-mail me for help at Linda@LindaBrakeall.com! We do two-day Visual and Verbal Workshops, (<u>Unlocking the Secrets of Success!</u>) corporate skill-shops, keynotes, seminars and one on-one coaching, but all that is secondary to helping you communicate better.

Warmly, **Linda**

Unlocking The Secrets of Successful Women in Business

We assume that if you're reading this book you are ready to move to the next level in your career and just need a boost.

We're so glad that you've chosen us to help. We'd like to share a story that popped onto the computer screen this week— *isn't e-mail wonderful?* — as we were writing.

A story . . .
An out-of-towner drove his car into a ditch in a desolated area. Luckily, a local farmer came to help with his big strong horse named Buddy. He hitched Buddy up to the car and yelled, "Pull, Nellie, pull!" Buddy didn't move. Then the farmer hollered, "Pull, Buster, pull!" Buddy didn't respond. Once more the farmer commanded, "Pull, Coco, pull!" Nothing.

Then the farmer nonchalantly said, "Pull, Buddy, pull!" and the horse easily dragged the car out of the ditch. The motorist was most appreciative and very curious. He asked the farmer why he called his horse by the wrong name three times. The farmer said, "Old Buddy is blind and if he thought he was the only one pulling, he wouldn't even try."

Why did we share that story? It says to us that there is strength in knowing that you are not alone. That's one of the reasons we write together.

The authors are bringing you information that is a compilation of personal and collected experience and anecdotes gathered from women friends over the last 20 years, observations made in various business venues where we have spoken, trained and consulted, and a fair amount of research. A new, but dear friend, Helena Douglas, who is in charge of all of the national outreach programs and conferences from Clemson University in South Carolina, says, "Women are always so willing to help and share!"

We promise you that while it won't be effortless, it will be worth the effort. We hope you'll read the whole book when time permits, but sometimes you need specific information *now*. We've laid it out so that you have easy access to what you want when you want it. Start with the tests and discovery exercises so that you'll know what you need to read first.

Our purpose is to help you re-view your life, knowledge and experiences and re-frame it in a way that is self-affirming and compels you to positive action. *Remember, you are not alone! We're pulling with you.*

Anna and Linda

PS: We solicit your input, feedback, corrections and comments which we will use it when we update this book. So keep those cards, letters and especially those e-mails comin'!

* * * * *

Contact the authors:

Anna Wildermuth
Personal Images Inc.
498 Hampshire
Elmhurst, IL 60126
630-530-9440
anna@personalimagesinc.com

Linda Brakeall
Phoenix Seminars
11 Arrow Wood, Suite 2A
Hawthorn Woods, IL 60047
800-662-7248
Linda@LindaBrakeall.com

I couldn't wait for success,
so I went ahead without it.
Jonathan Winters

Pretend that every single person you meet
has a sign around his or her neck that says,
"Make me feel important."
Mary Kay Ash

Unlocking The Secrets of Successful Women in Business

Key 1

Where Are You Now?

You send a message about who you are on the inside by how you dress, behave and carry yourself. It's easier on everyone — including you — if the message is consistent. Be consistent with who you are, what you wear, and consistent with the professional image that is required for your career or field. The way you walk into a room sends a clear message not only about who you are, but how you feel about yourself.

Each of us is unique. We may not all be "beautiful" in a traditional cover-girl sort of way, but who cares? Each of us can be well put-together, and project charm, style and charisma. We are happy to report that the rules have changed.

Many famous women that we consider role models go way outside the "traditional" rules and are still thought of as "beautiful."

🔑 Sophia Loren, still a sexy siren in her sixties, was told to get her big nose fixed, as was Barbra Streisand. They have each developed their own style and grace and no one mentions their noses these days.

🔑 People kept telling Rosie O'Donnell to slim down if she wanted to go anywhere in show biz. And we've all watched Oprah's struggles with weight. Last time we looked, no one confused either of them with Kate Moss but they were both doing pretty well.

🔑 Many super-models felt gawky and awkward growing up and when you look closely, many could never be described as "pretty"…but they're making a great living on their looks!

All of those women have learned how to "package" their professional image. You can too.

You want to feel confident when you walk into any situation and you want to know that you are presenting yourself appropriately. When you feel good about the way you look and sound professionally and personally, and know how to conduct yourself in most situations, it gives you the freedom to relax, be clear about your purpose and pursue your goals. Everyone knows it is important to make your first impression a good one. The only question is, how?

Before we go into more details, take the following brief tests to help you identify your strengths and find out where we can help you.

Unlocking The Secrets of Successful Women in Business
Is Your Appearance Up To Date?

In the first quick quiz, there are 16 questions divided into two sections. Answer yes or no.

1. ___ Have you worn your present hairstyle less than 2 years?
2. ___ Do you wear makeup?
3. ___ If # 2 is YES, are your makeup colors less than 2 years old?
4. ___ Can you do your everyday hair and makeup in less than 30 minutes?
5. ___ If you wear glasses, are your frames current?
6. ___ Do you have a color palette for makeup, hair and glasses?
7. ___ Are you comfortable when you walk into a room?
8. ___ Do you have a professional role model or mentor?
9. ___ Do you mirror any of her appearance?

Linda Brakeall and Anna Wildermuth

Is It Quick And Easy To Look Smart?

10. ___ Can you get dressed in less than 30 minutes?

11. ___ Can you choose a complete outfit in less than 30 minutes?

12. ___ Do you feel well dressed, comfortable and confident in most of your clothes?

13. ___ Do you have a standard professional "uniform" you wear at least once a week?

14. ___ Have you worn most of the clothes in your closet at least twice this year?

15. ___ Can you find a specific clothing item in your closet in five minutes or less?

16. ___ Does everything in your closet fit you comfortably?

17. ___ Do you have fewer than 3 colors besides black in your closet? (All shades of blue, etc., count as one.)

🗝 If you answered YES to 14 or more questions, you are already pretty well put together. Use this book as a refresher.

🗝 If you answered YES to 7-13 questions, this book will help you fine-tune your professional image.

🗝 If you answered YES to 6 or less questions, we've got the systems, secrets and know-how to have you looking and feeling great in no time.

Unlocking The Secrets of Successful Women in Business

How Do You Feel About Your Body?

Rate the following phrases from 1 to 5.

Example: If you are extremely satisfied with "What you see in the mirror," you'd rate the first question as a 5.

```
              1    2    3    4    5
Extremely                    Extremely
Unsatisfied                  Satisfied
```

A. What I see in the mirror. ___

B. The way I look in photos. ___

C. The way clothes look on me. ___

D. Shopping for clothes. ___

E. What I weigh. ___

F. With my height. ___

G. The shape of my body. ___

🔑 If you answered mostly with 3, 4 and 5's you are pretty comfortable with your body. You basically like yourself and the clothes you purchase feel good on your body

🔑 If your answers were mostly 1, 2 and 3's, you are unsatisfied with your body image and we are going to help you maximize your assets.

🔑 I (Anna) feel strongly that we are all perfect in our own way …but most of us have a few clothing challenges.

Linda Brakeall and Anna Wildermuth

How Are You Perceived When You Speak And Sell?

Use a scale of 1 to 5. (1 = "I need a lot of help!")
(5 = "I am awesome!")

A. When I speak professionally, (with clients, customers or peers) people pay attention. I know how to create a powerful presentation and I deliver it with panache. ____

B. I know I am persuasive because people usually co-operate with me. ____

C. When I explain things, I am brief and to the point. ____

D. I usually know what to do with my hands and body when speaking to more than a few people. ____

E. I speak with strength, confidence, conviction and power. ____

F. People usually believe what I tell them. ____

G. I've been told I'm magnetic or charismatic. ____

🗝 If you answered with mostly 4 and 5's, you communicate well. You might pick up a few new hints in here and if you have some we don't, send them to us.

🗝 If you answered with mostly 1, 2 and 3's, you'll find all the tips, tricks, techniques and *confidence* you need to make your presentation sound wonderful. Additionally, I'll (Linda) explain to you *why* things work the way they do. You'll be able to make dramatic progress in a short period of time.

Unlocking The Secrets of Successful Women in Business

Do You Know The Rules OF Business Etiquette And Communication?

True or False?

A. ____Your water and wine glasses and cup belong on the right side of your plate.

B. ____ Carefully slice a dinner roll in half before buttering.

C. ____ If you take a client to lunch, start discussing business right away because time is precious.

D. ____Leaving a voice mail message conveys how you do business.

E. ____ When prioritizing messages to return, leave the e-mail for last.

F. ____ Introductions have no particular rules. As long as everyone meets everyone, it's OK.

G. ____Ladies always initiate the handshake.

Answers: A-True, B-False, C-False, D-True, E-False, F-False, G-False

Linda Brakeall and Anna Wildermuth

Discovery Exercises

Presentations

Keep your answers in mind as you read the section on presentations.

A. In what situations do you have to deliver any kind of talk to more than one person?

B. When you see and hear someone else speak or present (either one on one, or to a group), what impresses you?

C. When you see and hear someone else speak, what offends and irritates you?

D. How do you go about creating a presentation? (Such as write it out and edit, or show up and pray.)

E. Whom do you need to persuade, sell or charm? And why? (Clients, customers, co-workers, family, friends?)

F. Where and when do you want to sound more knowledgeable, more powerful, more astute, and more sincere? Are there specific occasions? (Staff meetings, corporate meeting, conventions, and sales presentations?)

Charisma Corner

A. Watch people (solo or in groups) in a positive, happy mode and write down how they look.

B. Observe someone who is convincing and passionate about a subject. What does the body do (not just the words) to convince you?

C. Watch someone who is upset and or angry. Specifically, how does the body look?

D. Find someone who is apathetic, who doesn't care about anything. What does that body look like?

E. Observe people in person or on TV who speak with confidence, strength and power. What specifically conveys that confidence, strength and power?

> A man's got to do what a man's got to do.
> A woman must do what he can't.
> Rhonda Hansome

> It takes only one person to change your life
> – you!
> Ruth Casey

Linda Brakeall and Anna Wildermuth

Key 2

It's Not Easy Being A Successful Woman In Business!

It feels like you're walking a tightrope across a minefield. *Let's see:* I know that if I act too much like "one of the boys," they'll think I'm "butch" and "bossy" and they'll wonder if I'm going after their jobs. I also know that if I act like "one of the girls," they will never take me seriously. I'll be passed over for promotions, and someone else will take credit for my work.

If I dress well, they'll think I'm a fashion plate or a clotheshorse and will assume that I spend too much time shopping and not enough time at work. If I don't dress well, I have no personal pride or self-esteem. If I wear a lot of make-up they assume that I'm on the make. If I wear no make-up, I'm a dog. ***Grrrr.***

If I go to a corporate party or social event in a traditional, restrained navy blue suit like the guys do, they think I'm all business and no fun. If I go in a party dress, they assume I've slept my way to the top. Some women have successfully found their way through the minefield of the business world. So we know that it **is** possible, but one has to ask oneself:

What Is A Woman To Do?

We would all like to believe that the only thing that really matters is who we are, how we think, and how we perform our jobs. Unfortunately, we have seldom found that to be true. Example: In the promo before a television interview they flash a five second shot of the person to be interviewed. Don't you draw a lot of conclusions about that person *before* the interview begins?

You may not verbalize that impression but you ***know*** who works in a factory and who has a corner office. If you listen to the interviews you may discover that those initial impressions were not correct...or maybe they were. The point: Y*ou made a judgment in less than five seconds based on how someone looked.* Almost everyone does that.

When you heard that person speak, you drew a lot of other conclusions about where he or she grew up, social/economic/educational level and intelligence. Knowing that, one must conclude that the only sensible approach to professional success is to make your outside — both visually and verbally — match your inside. *Otherwise you are guilty of false advertising.*

Men, lucky men, have uniforms. They are called suits. Any man knows if he wants to climb the corporate ladder and wants to look important, that he merely needs to put on a navy or a gray suit, a white shirt and a burgundy tie. The rules have softened a bit, but those are still the basics even in the midst of business casual.

Linda Brakeall and Anna Wildermuth

You Need Some Version Of A Business Uniform.

For corporate ladder climbing, we recommend suits for women, too. The newest professional garb is called retro-glam. It's exaggerated and probably a fad but it does deliver a message. It has to do with powerful women in the old movies, like Rosalind Russell, Joan Crawford and Katherine Hepburn who were powerful *and* glamorous. And the basic business-wear was always a good suit. Not skirts or jeans and sweaters. Not polite little sweater sets over slacks. *Power suit* sends the message *powerful woman*.

You Ask, "How Do I Get Them To Take Me Seriously?"

Here are the Cliff Notes on that. Details later.

Lower your speaking voice if you're a soprano, by singing with the radio...*an octave lower.* Then start talking there. In just a few months, you'll have a lower voice most of the time. Most women can do this technique easily, but if your throat hurts when you do that, *stop it!* We don't want you scratching your vocal cords. I (Linda) have taken lots of classes over the years because I speak and sing, and learned many techniques but this is the simplest and fastest way to enrich your voice.

Eliminate, "I think" from your conversation.

Substitute:
- Research shows us
- It has been my experience
- Use statistics. *93 % of the workforce...*

Make less small talk in the office.

It's called "small" talk for a reason. And yes, you may make *some* small talk; you may even make a *lot* of small talk because it makes people comfortable. I think of small talk as social lubrication. Just don't *always* be the one to take full responsibility for maintaining the conversation with your peers.

Learn how to fight!

Learn how to disagree without necessarily being disagreeable. Most women are not socialized to argue, so we shut down when confronted. Practice with friends. It's a valuable life skill to be able to state your position and stand your ground without getting flustered, tearful or nasty.

Interrupt occasionally.

Interrupt when you have an important point to make and insist when necessary. They can't take you seriously if they don't know your opinion. Watch Cokie Roberts on This Week on Sunday mornings for a great role model of how to do it firmly and politely.

Smile a little less.

Many women smile frequently in order to be liked. Being respected is far more important. Of course you can smile. Just be aware that sometimes we smile inappropriately and it makes us look less than powerful. Watch network news anchors; they only smile occasionally.

Don't play hostess unless you are hosting.

It's fine to take your turn fetching coffee. Just don't turn into the amiable assistant who never makes VP.

Minimize "upspeak."

Upspeak makes statements sound like questions, such as, *"Hi, I'm Linda Brakeall?"*

Make statements more often than asking questions.

It will make you sound more confident and secure. That is a very attractive quality. Men often perceive confidence as the basis for authority.

Use statistical information to back up your premises.

Women are often – at least subliminally – questioned about "the facts." Make sure you have them at your command.

Don't let off-site conferences lead you astray!

Understand that many a career has been sidetracked, when the person wearing *casual* clothes, in a non-business setting, fell into *casual* conversation and forgot that her job was on the line.

Never say anything at a business function in the Caribbean that you would not say in the corporate boardroom. It all counts. In fact, it often counts more.

The commonly held, but seldom verbalized, thought is that the reason corporations take people "on vacation," or to a resort for a company conference, is to get a look at the real you. They want to see how you perform when your guard is down; if you act foolishly at cocktail hour; if you understand the meaning of the word "discretion." Truth be told, they are even observing your spouse or significant other.

This may be casual. This may be out of the office, but you are still being evaluated as a professional. That includes how you behave, what you say, and how you look. You can have fun, but ask yourself how you'd feel if you were videoed and put on the evening news. Would it hurt your career? (And go *very* easy on the alcohol. It not only frees you of inhibitions, it often frees you of employment!)

Learn to play golf, tennis, handball, or poker and to drink with the boys.

Pick one or two and learn to play well if you want to be around when important decisions are being made. No, you needn't be a cigar-chomping, hard-drinking, pot-bellied gambler. You merely need enough of those skills to be around the *guys,* **some of whom may be gals,** when decisions are being made. The important decisions are seldom actually made at the board meeting. They only report, and perhaps discuss, the decisions there.

It's not always a case of women being discriminated against.

It's often simply that *they* promote the people *they* know best and trust. Trust and credibility, on a person to person level, takes at least two years to build. You need to spend time with the people you want to trust you. Playing golf etc. takes time. Got it?

Linda Brakeall and Anna Wildermuth

Just for you . . .

What inspirations or insights did you get from this chapter?

What else do you need to know? We might be able to help. Email us. anna@personalimagesinc.com
Linda@LindaBrakeall.com

**Behind every successful woman ...
Is a basket of dirty laundry.
Sally Forth**

**I have a brain and a uterus, and I use both.
When people ask me why I am running as a woman,
I always answer, "What choice do I have?"
Patricia Schroeder**

**Never doubt that a small group of thoughtful,
committed citizens can change the world.
Indeed, it is the only thing that ever has.
Margaret Mead**

Unlocking The Secrets of Successful Women in Business

Key 3

Getting To The Top

In business, the professional field is becoming more level. Or at least, some of the huge-est (Linda's word) potholes have been filled. And yet when you examine the statistics, it is apparent that we still have a very long way to go.

The Stats:

A recent magazine article said:

🔑 About a handful of women run Fortune 500 companies at the end of the year 2000. Only one woman is among the best-paid CEO's in America.

🔑 There are less than 5% of women in any kind of corporate top spots, unless a woman CEO owns the company.

🔑 Only 15 % of the partners in the nations' top law firms are women.

🗝 Only 6% of department chairs in medical schools are women.

🗝 Only 6% of Hollywood directors are women.

🗝 We've elected a total of 34 women senators since 1789. We now have 13 female senators in the year 2001, and have had statistically insignificant female representation in congress since 1789.

🗝 In a co-gender discussion, women often get ignored, patronized, not taken seriously, or simply out-shouted.

🗝 Statistically we are still paid 2% to 20% less for similar work.

What's Wrong With This Picture?

If you ask most activist women, they would say that these things are done *to* them. There is a conspiracy to maintain the status quo. That cannot be argued. There is *always* a conspiracy to maintain the status quo because no one likes change. *And women are co-conspirators!*

Why are we co-conspirators?

We wear many hats. We are expected to be learned, savvy, astute professionals. Most of us have families, so we are called (at 3:25 pm most days) to nurture, soothe and support others. Most of us have been encouraged to put people ahead of things. So while *he* is working on a balance sheet, *she* is making nice.

And, by the way, we would really like to have a personal primary, soul-connected relationship with one other person. We tend to nourish that marriage or relationship, build up that ego and we sometimes denigrate our talents, or take second place in order to maintain a happy personal life. **You may choose to do** that at home, but continuously playing second fiddle to *anyone* at work will not fast-track your career.

We have to take some of the responsibility for not being in the top spots.

Some of it is a well thought-out, intentional decision, "I want to be home with my children for 10 years and that means that I'll have to play catch-up later."

Some of it is not well thought out. We often send unintended, non-verbal, but nonetheless, very real messages. And we can't blame the person who receives the message for believing what he or she is "told."

Like what?

Like, "I'm a girl. Don't take me seriously." Am I the only one who has seen supposedly high-powered women go into important meetings in pastel suits and flowered dresses with lace collars? Now, we all know that if you are already publicly acknowledged as powerful and smart, or if you own the company, you can make your own rules...*about everything,* including clothes. Statistically, that is improbable. **The verbal and non-verbal messages you send tell others who you are**. Those messages tell others how to treat you, whether you are in the workplace to earn a little extra money or to forge a career.

What else?

Women in general, are less likely to speak in public, or less likely to be *asked* to speak in public. At any rate, we usually get less practice. People think the people who stand up and make the points are the people with the power. Savvy women who want to get ahead learn to speak well and they speak often. They know how to persuade and convince others. (That's "selling!") **Public speaking and sales skills are not merely professional skills. They are essential life skills.**

And...?

We women talk about things like feminine intuition, which sound like we've not done our homework. How about a woman in the boardroom who "just knows that we ought to do X." No statistics, no reports, no reasons. *She just knows.* "Feminine intuition!" she says with a smile. And no one takes her seriously. The truth is, *she is probably right,* but that *approach* will not fly in the boardroom.

How can women effectively use their intuition in the boardroom?

A Harvard study a few years ago said that fifty percent of upper executive decisions are usually made quickly on gut reaction. Then those decisions are backed up by logic. Men tend to be better at positioning *the very same intuition-based, gut-level information* as logical, savvy and inevitable. As a woman in business, it's okay to talk about what your "gut" says because men have "gut reactions" too.

"Feminine intuition" is suspect. That gut and/or intuition is the sum total of all that you have absorbed, learned and observed over the course of your entire life. It's what you learned in school and at your mother, father or favorite sibling's knee. It is all the experiences you have ever had with people, things and events. You know an amazing amount of information! The information processing equipment you have between your ears is better than most computers.

You simply don't know all that you know because there is no index in a human being.

Unlocking The Secrets of Successful Women in Business

Conventional wisdom tells us that women usually read people better than that other gender. As a woman, you have a well-developed, extraordinary, built-in system for making good and quick decisions. High powered, multi-zillionaires often talk about how *their* intuition got them to their present position of wealth and power. Once you are in charge, you too, can talk about your intuition. In the meantime, here's a strategy:

When you initially "know" something, and can't back up your "gut," you will need to have phrases handy to buy you some time until you can put it all together. Phrases like: "I read a study recently that indicated..." *Whatever would back up your premise.* Or, "That reminds me of a situation at another company that ...." Anything that will give them a reason to consider your solution. And even if you're not sure, *act like you are.* Make up statistics if you are reasonably sure that they are conceptually correct. It's called "puffing" and men do it 87% of the time!

Historically, most women have not been good at persuading people to see it their way. You may have wonderful ideas, but if no one else buys in, your good ideas may die a premature death.

You can also convince people to draw a correct conclusion, that is, *your conclusion*, by guiding them through the process that helped *you* arrive at that conclusion. However, in this instance, you ask questions rather than make statements.

Example: You might try this tactic that uses everyday information to draw conceptually correct conclusions. Let's say you want to persuade a group that there is a business opportunity because more people are living past age 100.

> **You say:** I have no idea exactly how many people are more than 100 years old, but I see Willard Scott saying "Happy Birthday" to them on the *Today Show*. How many people do you think he says "Happy Birthday" to every day?

Someone says: "Five."

You say: So that's five times a day times five days a week times fifty weeks a year. What is that number?

Someone will have a calculator and say: "That's 1250."

You continue: "Can we assume that no more than 10 % would be likely to send in their birthdays? (Wait for the heads to nod in agreement.) So would it be reasonable to assume that there will be a minimum of 12,500 people passing the century mark this year?" *(Currently there are 3.8 million Americans over the age of 85.)*

That wasn't merely asking questions; that was teaching Socratically. You let the person you are trying to persuade come up with *your answers* by asking a series of the right questions. And all of a sudden they understand why you are excited when they see the reality of the opportunity. *And you have positioned yourself as a thoughtful, forward-thinking executive.*

As women, we communicate differently. Not better. Not worse. But definitely differently. Here's what Rosalind Sedacca, a business communication strategist has to say about the verbal gender gap:

Helping Business Women Bridge The Gender Communication Gap
Guest columnist Rosalind Sedacca

In the '60s and '70s thousands of women fought a hard battle in the workplace. The purpose was to prove what seemed like a fundamental point: that, beyond the physical, there are no intrinsic differences between women and men. The intention was certainly valid -- opening doors to occupations and executive positions that were gender restricted or out of reach in the past due to the infamous glass ceiling. However, as the doors to equality began to open, an interesting reality also became apparent. Men and women are really not the same – in their thinking, acting, communicating or in many other behaviors. The truth is, we can never be the same, nor should we strive to be. Consequently, it is imperative that we recognize and understand just what those innate differences are – and then learn how to use them to our best advantage.

Understanding Primary Gender Differences

Researchers who have studied human beings from infancy through adulthood have found some universal differences between the sexes. By understanding how these innate differences show up in our lives we can arm ourselves with the awareness and skills that enable us to accelerate through the business hierarchy with minimum stress and maximum success.

To simplify any conversation about gender dynamics, we need to make broad generalizations about males and females. While individual personalities and other factors all play a part in determining our behaviors, gender differences are significant enough for us to acknowledge, study and discuss. The primary difference between the genders is that men, in general, are *resolvers* and women are *relaters*.

Being resolvers, men focus on doing, taking action, finding solutions, getting things done and solving problems. As a result they are very *externally* focused.

As relaters, women focus on pleasing, communicating, making connections, understanding feelings, exploring emotions and being understood. As a result they are more introspective and *internally* focused.

Acclaimed author Deborah Tannen sums up these differences quite succinctly by pointing out that "women talk to establish *rapport* … while men talk to *report.*" According to Tannen, this means women use language in ways that develop relationships; men use language to tell people what they know. Our basic intentions and perspectives are different, and those differences play themselves out in a myriad of ways throughout our culture. This is complicated even further by the dichotomy of our internal versus external focus. "Mars/Venus" author John Gray says this difference is apparent very early on in children. When young boys have to deal with life problems, they tend to *act out*. They get more aggressive, even violent, and are likely to blame others for their dilemmas.

Gray notes that when young girls are faced with similar difficulties, they tend to *act in*. They get more introverted and usually blame themselves. This is why, according to Gray, 80% of the people in our prisons are men and 80% of the people in therapy are women.

Transcending Historical Challenges

So what happens when the externally focused *resolver* interacts with the internally focused *relater* in the workplace? Misunderstanding, mistrust and enormous confusion in our perceptions of how to behave, communicate and get things done. This is not surprising when you consider that females have been invading the male- dominated work environment for only a few short decades. Prior to the sixties and seventies women were relegated to a very narrow range of job possibilities: primarily as teachers, nurses, secretaries and sales clerks. Beyond these parameters the pickings were slim, the possibilities quite limited. As women accelerated their climb into the managerial and executive hierarchy, the differences in their approach to business – especially in terms of communication and relationship-building – became areas of contention at worst, and confusion at best.

In the male-focused business world both men and women agree on one thing: men have greater perceived credibility. They're more comfortable standing in their power as authorities. Women are fighting age-old perceptions to gain their credibility. While men are judged by the position of power they hold, women in our culture are often still judged by the presence they bring into a room. In many cases they have to earn their influence through means other than perceived authority. That translates into working harder to prove themselves through overcoming more obstacles, achieving higher goals and demonstrating skills that measurably boost the bottom line.

A fundamental principle of psychology notes that those they see as similar to themselves more readily influence people. Men have always taken this for granted when dealing with other men in business. Dissimilarity has become a major challenge for many career women who have trouble assimilating into the business world or corporate culture because they don't always know how to "play by the rules."

Honor Your Skills As A Relater.

When communication difficulties arise, use the **reap** formula for clarification:

R = **repeat** and review what you hear him say;
E = **empathize** with his feelings;
A = **acknowledge** the validity of his message, even if you don't agree; then
P = **persist** with patience until you can communicate and eliminate defensiveness -- with clarity and respect.

Reprinted with permission by Rosalind Sedacca, a business communication strategist, who speaks, trains and consults on women's business issues and gender communication dynamics. She can be reached at 561-588-5581, or talk2roz@aol.com.

Unlocking The Secrets of Successful Women in Business

What Else Do We Do As Co-Conspirators?

We give up our power without a fight!

We often give up our positions too easily when dealing with men because they sound so sure and confident. Don't assume that men are not willing to negotiate just because they make a statement, rather than asking for agreement or consensus. They may deliver *their opinion* with confidence and authority but that does not mean it is written in stone. Men simply tend to open negotiations from a position of power.

Women think differently!

> *Women tend to think out loud,*
> *and in the thinking process*
> *we investigate various options.*
> *That may <u>sound</u> as if we are vacillating.*

How does that work? Many women are external processors and *need to talk* in order to process the information. A professor explained the difference between internal and external processors to me (Linda). He said the internal processors get quiet and mull over the facts and eventually come to a conclusion. The external processors just start talking.

He said it's as if each thought comes out and goes up into the air like balloons that are over cartoon characters in the comics. After the external processor gets lots of balloons up there, she or he looks them over and thinks,

"Hmmm. Yes, I believe this one and that one. No, not that one. This is good. That's stupid! Maybeeee that one…"

The problem is that when we process our thoughts out loud in front of others, we can be accused of being wishy-washy, undecided, or flaky!

The internal processor went through exactly the same process as the external processor *but no one knew.* If you are an external processor, find a confidante, your assistant, or your cat, to listen to you think out loud behind closed doors until you find your opinion or conclusion. Then you can present a positive, well-thought-out statement to your audience.

Sometimes We Shoot Ourselves In The Foot Because We Don't Know How To Fight Or Disagree Without Being Disagreeable.

Most women simply don't like to fight.

Most of us didn't join the "debate club" in school. We haven't had a lot of practice at logically and unemotionally making our position understood. Most of us don't have the skill-set for comfortable confrontation.

It makes us mad when we get mad! Because we resist confrontation early, we tend to put our foot down only when we have exhausted every other possibility.

We tend to smooth things over until we can no longer stand it and then we blow. And people are surprised. We patiently wait for the other person to "get it" and make changes all by him or herself. We wait patiently for someone else to tell him or her.

We wait patiently for the situation to resolve itself without ever having to raise our voices. And then, *all of a sudden*, we run out of patience. And we fill up with anger. Not just a little anger. Not just a little aggravation. **Oh no!** We've been patient far past human tolerance so that *when we finally blow*, wounded, bleeding bodies are strewn about the floor. Finally we shriek our "request" as the office quivers and wonders, *"What's with her*? Where did *that* come from?"

We have to learn how to fight early and often.

Far better to be honest along the way. Make it clear immediately when things aren't working for you. As women, most of us really don't like conflict. Rather than stand toe to toe and fight it out, we tend to walk away… and just keep walking. In casual relationships, like a bad experience at a store, that works because there are lots of other stores where you can shop. But when it comes to a significant relationship, whether it's your spouse, your romantic interest, a co-worker, a child, or a boss we have to get better at speaking up!

We have to learn how to disagree without being disagreeable! Not violently, just assertively as soon as we are, shall we say, "miffed?" Why put off the inevitable? Do it while you still have a cool head, and avert major blow-ups later.

> "Lee, your report does not provide the tri-state sales statistics I need in order to do my report. Can you insert those numbers and get your report back to me by 3 pm today?"

> "Pat, when you're late for the staff meeting, it slows down the process. None of us have time for that. I'll expect you to be here prior to 8 am from now on."

Linda Brakeall and Anna Wildermuth

"If you can't say no within the relationship,
ultimately you will have to say no
TO the relationship."   Linda Brakeall

Translation: You have to learn how to fight if you want the relationship to continue. That's true at the office and at home. As long as you can discuss the issue, no matter how heatedly, the relationship has a chance to survive. When you can no longer talk it over, explore the problem and look for solutions, the relationship is vulnerable. If the lack of communication continues, the relationship is doomed.

"I don't believe that violence solves anything.
You better leave before I jump to a poor conclusion!"
Ally McBeal

Many conflicts are caused by simple misunderstandings.

One of you is talking about one thing and the other is talking about an entirely different subject. (Like the *very* old story of the minister changing his sermon at the last minute from an illustration about riding a motorcycle to an illustration about sex. His wife, who spent the morning teaching Sunday School, had only heard the motorcycle story. A church member chatting with the wife and the minister after services compliments the minister on his astute observations in his sermon. His wife says, "I don't know how astute he could have been. He only tried it once. He fell off because he was going too fast, and he's never done it since.") We all laugh hard at that one because similar things have happened to each of us.

That is called a parallel conversation. Both of you *think* you're talking about the same thing, but you're not. Without clarification, all kinds of ugly things could evolve. You know it's a parallel conversation when it starts to make no sense at all.

Unlocking The Secrets of Successful Women in Business

That is the time to say, "Time-out! I think we're talking about two different things. I'm talking about riding a motorcycle. What are you talking about?" Many times that is all it takes; a quick time-out for clarification.

We, as a gender, need some help when it comes to conflict. We would really prefer everyone to just "get along." A fellow speaker, Carter Johnson, shares some insights about conflict management styles.

How Do *You* Deal With Conflict?
Guest columnist Carter Johnson

Chances are you have a certain style for managing conflict. Perhaps you're a skillful negotiator, a compromiser, or a dictator whose tolerance for conflict is minimal. Here are five styles of conflict management, and a quick quiz.

– **Forcing**. All or nothing. Only one party can win, forcefully if necessary.
– **Avoiding**. The avoider will stay out of it.
– **Yielding**. The strategy is to withdraw, let the other party win.
– **Compromising**. The emphasis is on give-and-take, the agreement partially satisfying each.
– **Problem solving**. A collaborative solution is reached by a time-consuming process that uncovers and satisfies the fundamental concerns of each of the parties

Which style would work best for each of these situations? (Hint: there are 2 for each style.)

1. Wage negotiations with a union.

2. As a user of financial reports, you have become involved in a conflict between the controller's office and top management.

3. This afternoon's management meeting has been called to determine space requirements in a new office building. Arguments are heated. Recommendations must be submitted by the end of the day.

4. 50% of a product has been rejected by quality control. Changes must be made immediately and your subordinates disagree on what should be done.

5. You have an argument going with marketing, which is committed to a huge advertising campaign for product features that you feel are impractical.

6. A festering personality conflict has been hampering productivity among your subordinates.

7. Two top managers are having a big fight. You have a third opinion, but you know neither of them will like it.

8. You know your people will react negatively to a new company policy, but you also know it's in the company's best interests.

9. You are involved in a heated conflict with another department head, but you'll need her support next month for a proposal of your own.

10. You need agreement on the application of new office procedures. Your people have conflicting opinions.

Forcing is best used when quick, decisive action is vital, such as in #4. It's also necessary in situations where unpopular, but necessary, policies or practices must be implemented (#8). If a situation is not critical, a forcing position can make lasting enemies.

Avoiding conflict is a good posture in situations where you are an outsider (#2) or where you are relatively powerless (#7). It's also appropriate when people (or you) are too emotional and need to cool down. In the long run, however, consistently avoiding conflict is a negative, branding you as someone with few opinions and little to contribute.

Yielding can be very effective when you recognize that the issue is much more important to the other party than to you (#5) or you want to gain allies (#9). If you're going to yield, choose the right issues and at the right times, before you've become too committed to your approach.

Compromising is often the appropriate mode when both parties have equal power, such as in the union negotiations (#1). It also may be necessary when under time constraints (#3). Remember, however, that compromising always leaves each party somewhat disappointed, with unresolved issues that are sure to arise again.

Problem solving is the best mode for long-term results, but it doesn't work in all circumstances. It works well when resolving personality conflicts (#6) and when cooperation and commitment are needed (#10).

The easiest conflict trap is to feel constrained to one method because it's the one that comes naturally. An understanding of alternatives, coupled with some quiet thinking prior to a confrontation, can result in a posture that can be most effective. Some conflict styles back up one another. Thus, if problem solving doesn't succeed, compromising, forcing or yielding can be used.

Unlocking The Secrets of Successful Women in Business

The final word: conflict resolution is not always possible. Remember, the object is to manage conflict, instead of letting conflict manage you.

Article reprinted with permission by Carter Johnson, Buying Time Seminars. Carterj636@aol.com

> When women are depressed
> they either eat or go shopping.
> When men are depressed,
> They invade another country.
> Elayne Boosler

Sometimes We Shoot Ourselves In The Foot Because We Want People To Like Us.

That's natural and that's why some of us smile too much. Let me be clear: smiling is fine. Smiling is *good*. But there is smiling that is done primarily in order to ingratiate oneself with the powers that be. That is not good. *All people do not have to like you all the time.* Respect is far more important. Can you imagine General Colin Powell smiling all the time? (Why don't we have a well-known woman general to use as an example?)

> I had to learn to separate my feelings for a person
> from his/her performance on the job.
> Debbie Fields, Mrs. Field's Cookies

Save the "sandwich" for lunch!

An example of unsuccessful discipline in the pursuit of being liked and being "nice" is popularly called the *sandwich technique.* You say something nice to the employee, you state the problem, and then you reassure the person. Mary Kay Ash, as in

Mary Kay Cosmetics, created this and it works very well with women, but it seldom ever works with men.

The Sandwich: "John, I have always valued your contribution to the team but this report isn't up to your usual standards. Could you incorporate statistics to back up your findings and tell us the impact on the bottom line? The rest of the report is fine."

Most men, and some women, rarely hear the problem that was politely "sandwiched" in the middle. John heard: "Valuable contribution." John heard: "Report is fine." So John does nothing. When you eventually confront him, he'll tell you what *he heard, ("You said the report was 'Fine.'"*) and he'll be confused when you are angry.

You can still be pleasant, but when the report has to be done over, it has to be done over. No personal or moral judgment is required and definitely no apology.

"John, there are two problem areas in this report. Back up your premise in part one with statistics. How many X's are we making? How many Y's are we behind? In part two, explain how these changes affect the bottom line. Spell it out. The rest of your report is fine. I need those two corrections by noon tomorrow."

Often when disciplining an employee or a direct report, we tend to soften the criticism, because we don't want to hurt anyone's feelings. *And they might not like us if we're too direct.*

In the workplace, it is far more important that the job get done properly and on time. You're not there to win Miss Congeniality. If you'd like to wear a banner across your bosom, let it say: **Perfection is not required. Excellence is expected.** That will earn you respect.

Unlocking The Secrets of Successful Women in Business

**If you just set out to be liked, you would be prepared
to compromise on anything at any time,
and you would achieve nothing.
Margaret Thatcher**

Just for you . . .

List 3 actions steps that will help you progress professionally.

1.

2.

3.

What do you need to STOP doing in order to get to the top?

What inspirations or insights did you get from this chapter?

What else do you need to know? We might be able to help.
Email us. anna@personalimagesinc.com
    Linda@LindaBrakeall.com

You gain strength, courage, and confidence
by every experience in which you really stop
to look fear in the face.
You must do the thing which you think you cannot do.
Eleanor Roosevelt

Linda Brakeall and Anna Wildermuth

Key 4

Unlocking The Secrets Of Charm And Charisma In Business, In Sales, In Speaking And In Person!

My (Linda's) favorite definition of charisma is,
   "A special quality of leadership that captures the imagination and inspires unswerving allegiance and devotion."

Who wouldn't want "unswerving allegiance and devotion," especially if you are trying to persuade someone?

My favorite definition of charm is,
   "The quality of pleasing, attracting or fascinating."

Anyone who can command unswerving allegiance and devotion and can attract, please and fascinate others simply has to have an advantage in business. And anywhere else, too!

At our two-day workshops, people often laugh when I say that I do charisma implants. But I have discovered the elements that comprise charm and charisma and you can learn those elements

Unlocking The Secrets of Successful Women in Business

to use in sales, at work and at home. (Or at least enough of the elements to make you more effective.)

Just take a moment and think about someone you know, or know of, who has charm and charisma. *Really.* Think about a specific person. Got one?

Now jot down what it is that you find appealing about that person. Just 3 or 4 things. Quickly, don't think too much!

1. _____

2. _____

3. _____

4. _____

**Life is what we make it,
always has been, always will be.
Grandma Moses**

Linda Brakeall and Anna Wildermuth

Let Me Tell You What I Suspect Is On Your List, At Least In Some Version.

A. **The person who is described as having charm and charisma usually makes very good eye contact.** "She always looks me right in the eye when she's talking to me."

B. **Charming and charismatic people make themselves even more likeable by mirroring and pacing.** It's a natural phenomenon that you can imitate. You may not be familiar with those terms but you quickly feel very *comfortable* with a charming and charismatic person.

C. **Charming and charismatic people are usually described as "high energy."** They are frequently asked: "Don't you *ever* get tired?"

D. **Integrity shines in the thoughts, words and especially the actions of a charming and charismatic person.** You would trust this person with your family, your secrets or your money.

E. **Charming and charismatic people are congruent.** Their eyes, body, vocal tone, and the way they dress, all validate their words.

F. **Charming and charismatic people are comfortable with their bodies when they speak.** They know what to do with their hands and they look confident and natural.

G. **Charming and charismatic people have mastered the art of small talk.** Small talk helps others feel comfortable and when others are comfortable around you, they think you are delightful!

H. Charming and charismatic people are likeable and fun! They have a well-developed sense of humor, they don't easily fluster and are just plain enjoyable to be around. You'd invite a charismatic person to your party.

I. Charismatic women have fun when they lose their train of thought. It happens to everyone at one time or another. Lighten up!

J. Projecting your charm and charisma in sales situations and interviews. Getting people to like you and trust you quickly is essential when you're selling a product or selling yourself in order to get a job.

You can incorporate these ten simple elements into your personal style so that people will believe that you, too, have charm and charisma. Often it is merely a matter of making the inner you visible on the outside. Or, as the old saying goes, **"Fake it till you make it!"** Stay with me as I take you through the A, B, C's of charisma.

>She can who thinks she can,
>and she can't who thinks she can't.
>This is an inexorable, indisputable law.
>Henry Ford

>Laugh and the world laughs with you.
>Cry and you cry with your girlfriends.
>Laurie Kuslansky

A. The Person Who Is Described As Having Charm And Charisma Usually Makes Very Good Eye Contact.

Good eye contact jump-starts charisma and is relatively easy for about 70% of us; the other 30% have to work at it. If it is normally difficult for you to look at people when you are thinking, be especially well prepared for interviews, important sales calls etc., so that you can simply deliver the information and you don't have to think and create it as you talk. Thus, you'll be better able to maintain eye contact.

It is essential that you look at and listen attentively when the other person is talking so that they feel you are *really* listening to what they have to say. We all love good listeners, don't we?

No one listens to you until they feel heard by you!

Paying attention and giving positive feedback through good eye contact is essential to charm, charisma, sales and everyday communication at work and at home.

Even if you find it uncomfortable at first, try it. You'll be amazed at how much warmer people will become around you. My good friend Carol, gazes at me as I speak, as if she is trying to read my very soul. I love being in her company because when I get that kind of focused, rapt attention I feel like the most fascinating person in the world. You automatically like anyone who makes you feel like that!

Besides loving the attention, people tend to think that those who have good eye contact are "stronger." **If you are really trying to influence someone, focus both of your eyes on his/her left eye.** That will access the more receptive right brain.

B. Charming and Charismatic People Make Themselves Even More Likeable By Mirroring And Pacing.

Ever noticed two people in love at a dinner table? They could be an image and a mirror. Hence the name. People who are in "sync" do it all the time. You can do it first to become friends faster because people will do things for friends that they would not do for strangers.

How to mirror:

The two of you should be almost mirror images. While you are selling, presenting, or interviewing, sit or stand the way the other person sits or stands. Arrange your legs and arms to match the other person. Lean in or out or sit sideways to match their movements. Maybe not exactly, but closely, and not too suddenly or obviously. Don't worry; they won't catch you!

I (Linda) teach mirroring in sales classes. I also mention that it is effective in dating situations. After such a class a man came up to me who was — *how shall I put this?* — **not** a Mel Gibson clone. He really was not an attractive man. Nice, bright, but not attractive. He told me he had been using this mirroring technique for the past year off and on.

One night at a bar, he saw a very attractive lady. He knew that if he approached her, he would be turned down flat. He walked to the other side of the bar where he was in her direct line of sight. He mirrored her every action. If she picked up her drink, he did too. If she turned sideways, he did too. He did not stare. He did not flirt. He said this went on for over an hour. At one point he looked up and there she was — at his side. She said, "Have we met before? You look so familiar." They started talking and had a nice conversation. He told me if he had tried a direct approach, that conversation would have never happened. Such is the power of mirroring!

How do you use this professionally? At any initial meeting, mirror the body positions of the person you want to influence. You can also mirror smiling and their vocal tone. You continue to mirror as you build rapport through small talk for the first five to ten minutes. When you believe that you have "connected," you can test your perception by initiating a move such as leaning in or leaning back, crossing your legs, or repositioning your arms. If the other person mirrors *you*, you are in sync and then you can start to discuss the important issues. Until you reach that stage of connection, your efforts at persuading are not likely to succeed.

How to pace:

The two of you should speak at a similar speed. If he or she talks a mile a minute, you better speed up or the other person will be bored. If he or she speaks s l o w l y, then you better slow down or you will be perceived as "slick." Watch how the other person breathes. Breathe at the same speed. Mirroring and pacing are two sides of the same coin and they work together. This is so effective it's almost scary!

Have you even been really angry and upset about a product and called customer service

and someone said, "Calm down!"
Isn't that infuriating?

You *know* he or she wouldn't tell you to calm down if he or she really understood what you were angry about. When you are that angry, you want someone to be angry *with* you and *for* you.

I remember one of those times when grocery prices went up suddenly and all the shoppers were cranky. Standing in a grocery line among all those unhappy people, you could *feel,* even when no one actually said anything, that everyone was on a short fuse. Then I heard the checkout clerk yelling, "$5.98 for a pound of coffee. That's outrageous! How can they sleep at night? Two dollars and twenty-five cents for a box of crackers? What are these things made of?" And on he went, yelling about item after item. At first we were all shocked, then amused and finally we were all laughing so hard that tears were streaming down our faces.

That young man was pacing with us and mirroring our unhappiness. He started right where we were. We were outraged at the prices! *He got outraged with us and for us.* He was so outraged that finally we lightened up. Pacing is all about going emotionally or physically to the other person's place or point of view, aligning with them, by doing what they are doing (mirroring) and at their speed and intensity (pacing). After we knew *he knew* we were upset, we could lighten up because we felt understood. And we did. Once we were calmed down, he resumed his work without the theatrics.

Why do pacing and mirroring work?

People like people who are like themselves. Fast, slow, bright, dim, calm or angry. One thinks, "I am a wonderful person! *And if you are like me,* you must be wonderful, too."

Linda Brakeall and Anna Wildermuth

C. Charming And Charismatic People Are Usually Described As "High Energy."

How do you project high energy?

- Stand tall, shoulders back, head up!
- Walk briskly.
- Sit forward in your chair.
- Talk a little more quickly.
- Move quickly and with purpose even when you're only heading for the copier or the ladies room.
- **Never say: "I'm tired."** You are always ready for anything! I don't care how you *feel*, but you never say it. Think: Perky!
- Often be willing to go, do, and try new things. Be adventurous. "Let's go there! I've never been there before and I'll try anything once!"

The phrase, "working mother," is redundant.
Jane Sellman

D. Integrity Shines In The Thoughts, Words, And Especially The Actions Of A Charming And Charismatic Person.

People do business with people they trust. Make it easy to trust you. Integrity is not only being trustworthy but also *appearing* trustworthy. People who send mixed messages are incongruent. And when you are not congruent, people don't trust you. (We'll handle congruence next.) And you cannot persuade, influence or sell to people who do not trust you.

You never indicate by word or deed that you are willing to take ethical shortcuts. *Never.* If someone says: "Well, everybody fudges a little on income taxes." Keep quiet if you can't disagree wholeheartedly.

Give examples, or tell stories, to illustrate your integrity. You might say, "Some people (or companies) take shortcuts on this part. I just can't do that. A sale today is worth far less to me than establishing a relationship that will serve us both for years."

You talk about the time your mom found an unexplained pack of gum in your pocket and marched you right back into Wal-Mart to return it. And she grounded you for a week to make sure you learned your lesson.

Telling an unpleasant truth also signals integrity.

If you are in sales, this is an important concept. (And *we are all in sales at work and at home. Try to get a kid to clean his or her room. That's selling!*) Unless you are selling products that cost less than ten dollars, your prospect is already thinking: "Omigod! That's a lot of money!" So if you say it first, you will appear truthful and non-slick. (Which of course, you are.)

Say something like this: "The fact of the matter is that no one wants to spend $$$$ on a phone system. That's a lot of money! (Pause) But what are the alternatives? More personnel? Missed calls? More hostile customers? So actually, it just might be the best investment you'll make this year."

What is another "unpleasant truth" in your business?

Sometimes a bad market (for your product or industry) is the unpleasant truth. *PSSST!* They've already heard about the bad market. Maybe your best advice is, "Don't buy right now, the market's not in your favor." Hearing you actually say the words out loud sets you apart from all the other Pollyanna sales reps they've talked to. And almost instantly you seem trustworthy.

Perhaps you remember 1981 and '82 when interest rates spiked at 22%, in some parts of the country and caused the two worst years in real estate since the great depression. 1981 was the year that I (Linda) *chose* to sell real estate. *I chose to!* In the worst marketplace since the great depression!

1981 was not a good year to sell your home!

While that obviously does not speak well of my intelligence, I learned to work hard in that marketplace because I didn't know that it was supposed to be easy. I was Rookie of the Year that year and subsequently was usually in the top five in a company of 250 sales people while I was selling real estate.

1981 was not a good year to sell your home. Prices were low and interest rates were high, and yet we still got calls from people who wanted to sell their homes and move up to a bigger home, because it was a wonderful time to buy. One could always refinance when rates came down.

Time after time, I would do a market analysis, come up with a realistic listing price and probable sales price and I would tell the seller the very unpleasant truth: "Mr. and Ms. Jones, you've only been in this house a few years. I can't tell you that it makes any financial sense for you to sell at this time if this is a discretionary move. You will probably have to bring money to closing *if* we can sell this property. My best advice would be to either stay put for year or two until the market picks up, or buy a bigger house now and find renters for this house until it makes sense to sell so you can at least break even."

Now that was a *very* unpleasant truth. In essence, I was saying: "On the off chance that I can sell this property, you will not make any money on it. You will have to pay money out of your pocket to get this house sold. Why would you do that?"

And more often than not, in a week or two the sellers would call me back to sell their house. I would charge them more than the going rate because I knew I'd need extra money for marketing with so many houses on the market. And they'd pay it.

The first few times this happened, I asked why they wanted *me* to sell their house when everyone else was far more anxious than I to get the listing. They said, "The other brokers made us all kinds of outrageous promises. We know it's a bad market and this won't be easy. We know we'll have to bring money to the table to get out from under this house. And you were the only one who told us the unvarnished truth."

I learned a valuable lesson in sales. Make that two lessons.

1. Tell the unpleasant truth. It projects integrity and sets you apart from the crowd.
2. If you can get results, when most people can't, they'll pay you more money!

E. Charming And Charismatic People Are Congruent!

You are congruent when your eyes, your body, your voice and your attire all match your words.

When you are congruent, people not only believe you, they trust you. I'm sure you've met people that you just didn't trust. And often you're not exactly sure why. You think to yourself: "No, it wasn't what she said. That all made sense. But something about her didn't hit me right. I just was not comfortable." The problem all too often is "congruence," or the lack thereof.

> If you say: "I'm excited!" and look like you are ready to fall asleep, that is incongruent.

> If you say: "I'm happy!" and your smile radiates throughout your eyes, face and body, you are believable and that's congruent. Or, as I am fond of saying:

"If you're having a good time, notify your face!"

Let me give you an example. You make a sales call on Mr. Jones and you immediately wonder why the atmosphere is so uncomfortable. You say to yourself, "What have I done? What have I said?" It could be that Mr. Jones just isn't comfortable *...about something else.* For instance, he might not be feeling well. Perhaps he had an argument with someone, and while trying to maintain professional decorum with you, he is trying simultaneously to suppress rage. You may not see overt hostility, but you feel that he is not 100% there. And you wonder: "What aren't you telling me? Is something wrong with *me*? With the project? Are you trying to get rid of me?"

Unlocking The Secrets of Successful Women in Business

Chances are, it has nothing to do with you. Or with Jones' trustworthiness. But unless he takes a moment to explain the *disconnect* for you, you won't trust him.

Make sure if <u>you</u> are distracted, to explain it a little, so people won't feel that way about you. And the operative words here are "a little." Example: "Forgive me if I'm distracted, we had a small crisis just before you got here."

Exercise: Does all that sound confusing? Try the following exercise and see if it starts to make sense.

If you have a friend handy, do this exercise with her. If not, you can do it alone with a mirror. Read the following phrase: "I just adore New Year's Eve!"

Say it the first time with your eyes sparkling and your face smiling, feeling like a happy, wiggly puppy. That's congruent. Now say it again as you think of something sad. That's not congruent. Get the difference?

Try these with or without congruence.

Let your friend, a small group or your mirror tell you if you were believable. Did you get the answer you expected?

1. I'd like to vacation at the South Pole.
2. Winter is my favorite season.
3. The Cubbies are a great team!
4. I can't wait to sky dive!
5. I'm really scared!
6. I have a wonderful time riding horses.
7. I'm looking forward to my next roller coaster ride!

8. Presentations are the best part of my job!
9. ***Extra credit:*** Wear unpressed chinos, a polo shirt and beat up tennis shoes and say: "I'm a successful executive on the fast-track to becoming CEO of this company." *Did anyone believe you?*

If being congruent doesn't come naturally to you, you may have to practice a bit.

Find a partner who will give you brutally honest feedback for a week or two. For those of you who tend to be "poker-faced" and "dead-pan," this may be a challenge and you will need a very good coach who will observe, monitor and let you know when your eyes, words, body and face are not congruent. It is especially important for you to learn to externally emote, and dress, so that people will receive the right message.

Learning to be congruent may be a bit of a stretch for some of you, but I promise no one has ever died in the process of learning how to do this. So be brave and get on with it! People will like you more, your business and personal life will improve, and you'll probably win the lottery! (OK, so I just made up the last part!)

> **Our biggest problem as human beings is not knowing that we don't know.**
> **Virginia Satir**

F. Charming And Charismatic People Are Comfortable With Their Bodies When They Speak!

Do you have "too many hands?"

Or you don't know what to do with them? Did you know that when John F. Kennedy was running for his first elected office he was so nervous that he kept one hand in his pocket most of the time because it was always shaking?

A CEO I know almost always has a pen in one hand and a glass of water in the other when he speaks. It took me years to figure out why. He doesn't know what to do with his hands so he keeps them occupied with a pen and a glass of water. It looks natural and seldom detracts from his speech. You too, can hang on to a pen or a glass of water; just don't "fiddle" with it.

If you tend to wander. . .

...aimlessly about the office (classroom or stage), try standing in one place most of the time. I learned how to do this the hard way. One of my banking clients sponsored me to speak at an Annual Realtor Luncheon in Savannah, Georgia. They told me not to take it personally if people left the country club early because Realtors are busy people and usually leave early.

I got to the club and observed that the room was very long and narrow. There were no risers and no stage. The only mic was attached to the lectern and it had a 6-foot cord. Projecting ahead to my speech I knew that standing there, unable to move away from the lectern, I would feel like a tethered sacrificial goat.

My future was not looking bright. I'm a speaker who racks up a lot of miles. I walk and talk and physically touch people. (If only there was a program for frequent speaker miles.) *And they want me to stand still at a lectern for 45 minutes?* No can do! At least not if there is any other possibility.

I spoke with the manager. "Do you have a longer cord for the mic?" He did. After my introduction, I took my mic out into the audience, but I still didn't feel connected. I couldn't see the back of the room so I knew they couldn't see me. I climbed up on a chair just to see the far reaches of the room. I said, "Hi!" to those in the back and they were amused and delighted. *So I stayed there for 45 minutes.*

No one left that day because for the first time, they could see and hear the speaker. The Realtor Association learned how to keep their audience and I learned that one could indeed stand still if properly motivated.

You can learn not to wander, too. Pick a story or an anecdote that you know pretty well. Climb up on a chair and deliver it. (In order to preserve some semblance of dignity, you might want to do this behind closed doors.) You'll quickly find that yes indeed, you can stand still and talk if the alternative is falling off the chair and breaking your neck. Once you understand that it can be done, you'll be able to stand still with your feet firmly on the floor the next time you want to demonstrate power.

You say, "What do I do with my hands?"

Relax! You are only self-conscious about your body, which often manifests itself as "too many hands," or physical discomfort, when you are nervous and unsure. If you know your topic inside out, tell me all about it. Stay involved and focused on your message and forget about the messenger; i.e. *you*. If you are intently focused on the message, you'll forget about your own personal discomfort and your presentation/platform skills will develop. And that includes feeling comfortable with your body when you are presenting. If you don't know your presentation or speech inside out, cram until you do. Tape record it and play it over and over.

> *Nothing promotes physical, emotional and mental confidence more than being well rested, well nourished and <u>knowing</u> that you know your stuff!*

We all learn incrementally.

So take it one step at a time. You weren't born knowing how to ride a bike or drive a car and no one is born knowing how to speak. You have to start wherever you are. If you need notes, use notes. If you need something to hang onto, hang on! If you tend to stand rigidly in one spot, behind a lectern, be brave and take just one step away the next time, and see how it feels. Take the pressure off yourself!

Don't expect perfection.

Even the pros aren't perfect. They screw up more often than most folks would believe. *I know I do!* And they've learned to live with it. Just do it! You'll get better, I promise. It is all too easy to strive for perfection and feel miserably inadequate because you are not a born orator. I'll let you in on a few trade secrets. Speakers' bureaus, which act as booking agents for speakers, tell me they will book speakers who have *either* wonderful content *or* great platform skills. Yes, speakers' bureaus would love to get both, but they will settle for *either*. If you know your topic inside out, you'll be able to make do until your skills match your content. I'm telling you this because I want you to know that perfection is not required.

G. Charming And Charismatic People Have Mastered The Art Of Small Talk.

Read a lot so you have something to talk about, but don't ramble on and on if no one's interested. *Please don't be a Cliff Claven from Cheers!* who could boringly babble on for ten minutes about a postage stamp.

Create short comments or questions that can open conversations.

I don't know about you, but I hate cocktail parties! Hate 'em! A lot! But I have to go to a fair number of them. *(Given my "druthers" – that's a southern word for "choice"– I'd turn around and go home, but one doesn't do that, does one?)* If I don't recognize anyone in the room, I look for another person who's alone. I walk over, and say: "Hi! I'm Linda Brakeall. I do wish I were better at these cocktail-party things but I just hate small talk!"

Many a time, the other person has said: "Oh, me too!" and a wonderful conversation has ensued. "I hate cocktail parties and small talk!" has become my standard icebreaker. Use mine or create one of your own.

Don't interrogate, but look for areas of common interest by asking questions about other people, and they will find you likeable and fascinating - and that is always fun.

One of my friends often says to a new acquaintance: "So, tell me all about *you*!" And people tend to do so. While I personally find this approach activates my gag reflex, I've seen her in action and I know it works. People usually think she is a scintillating conversationalist although her comments often sound like: *"Hmmm," "Oh?" "Really!"* and, *"Tell me more!"*

Unlocking The Secrets of Successful Women in Business

An old trick to start a conversation is to give a compliment.

The new variation turns it into a three-part process that goes like this and has never failed me.

1. Carefully observe and find something worthy of a compliment. Don't be obvious. (Except for men's ties. You can compliment almost every man in the room on his tie and each one will beam. Just don't let them hear you talking to the other men about *their* ties.) Make the compliment: *"What an unusual brooch! I really like it..."*

2. Back up the compliment with a "because" phrase because studies prove that people tend to believe anything that comes after the word *because*. *"... because it reminds me of one I saw in a museum."*

3. Follow with a question to engage the other person in conversation: *"Is it a family treasure?"*

A good time-tested resource for developing small talk is the classic book: How To Win Friends And Influence People.

> When Harvard men say they have graduated
> from Radcliffe, then we've made it.
> Jacqueline Kennedy Onassis

> Nature never repeats herself,
> and the possibilities of one human soul
> will never be found in another.
> Elizabeth Cady Stanton

Linda Brakeall and Anna Wildermuth

H. Charming And Charismatic People Are Likeable And Fun!

Develop your sense of humor.

It's a muscle that may need a workout if you are perceived as humor-free. Watch funny movies. Read funny stories. Collect cartoons. Smile and lighten up! Unless you are a brain surgeon, no one will die if a little mistake is made. Remember "fun" is part of charm and charisma.

Example: "I suspect a tree gives its life every time I fill out these forms. I suppose it would be environmentally correct for me to stop submitting paperwork. ...and I'd get home earlier, too!" Then *smile!* That's not a knee-slapper, but it is an amusing aside that lightens the atmosphere while getting paperwork done.

If verbal wit is not your long suit, maybe you could start collecting cartoons to share. *Not a lot.* That's boring. But one cartoon that amuses you each week? That could be fun. "Look at what I found in the New Yorker. Isn't that funny?" Fun by association. As long as they laugh when they are around you, they will think you're responsible.

My very favorite cartoon is from the Far Side. In the background we see a man walking under a piano suspended by a rope from a third floor window. In the foreground we see an elderly man sitting at a computer with his hand poised over the **SMITE** button. Caption: *God at his computer.* Makes you think, doesn't it? And perhaps chuckle, too?

> The hardest years are those
> between ten and seventy.
> Helen Hayes

Prepare people to laugh.

Many analytical types such as accountants, tax lawyers, and detail people are *very* funny. Their humor tends to be dry, deadpan humor, which no one expects, so people are often afraid to laugh

If you fall into this category, you must prepare people to laugh by "telegraphing the punch" and warning them that a "funny" is coming. They are often not sure if you meant to be amusing. They think, "Wouldn't it be awful if I laughed and you meant it seriously?" They don't want to laugh *at* you, and they are not at all sure if they are laughing *with* you... So they don't laugh at all. Next time, try one of these:

- Giggle, chuckle, or at least smile, just a bit before you deliver that funny line.
- Or say: "This is sooo funny . . ."
- Or deliver the line, then smile and wait quietly for them to catch on.

Even if you are a gifted joke or storyteller, it is inevitable that one day you will tell a funny joke or story and no one will laugh.

No one. The room will shriek silence! Or a client will gaze at you blankly. It is imperative that you are ready for that to happen, because it will.

When I do a seminar tour, I can tell the same funny story twelve times in four weeks. Three times, the people in the room will laugh so hard they'll have tears in their eyes and clutch their stomachs. Seven times, they'll laugh and enjoy it. And at least two times they'll silently stare at me as if I were an oil painting.

The first time no one laughed, I panicked! I soon found the words to say that would permit me to go on. I always think of Johnny Carson, who was sooo good at turning faux pas into fun. So now when that happens to me, I say:

"Some of these I do just for me!"

"You know, that's my cat's favorite story!"

"It looks like I need a new writer!"

"Did anyone get that one? Will you explain it to the folks around you?"

Your comeback line doesn't have to be funny. It merely needs to be *available* so that you will not feel like a silly fool and you will be able to go on. So pick one of those or write your own. Memorize it and be prepared.

Anything unusual is fun!

Perhaps you keep a jar of unusual candy on your desk to share. Ordinary candy will do, but something unusual sends a message that *you're* unusual. That's fun! ("Isn't this Himalayan Triple Fudge Truffle absolutely decadent?") And it gives people a reason to stop by and get better acquainted. And as they know you better, you become more likeable.

"Fun" is a state of mind!

Hang around people who are "fun" and watch what they do. What do they do, or say, that you could adapt?

I. Charismatic Women Have Fun When They Lose Their Train Of Thought!

They think, or *pretend to think,* it's funny. Keep in mind that the people you're selling to, speaking to or presenting to are only human. *Well.... most of them!*

If, for example, you are telling a story and by the end of the story have forgotten why you're telling it, 'fess up! "Now I'm sure when I started this story I had a reason for telling you. Does anybody remember where I was going with this?" It always amazes me that someone was listening far more carefully to what I was saying than I was. Really! I've used that line in one on one conversations and from the platform with 500 people. And someone *always* helps me get back on track. Or they don't. And we laugh about *that*.

Second tip: Take a deep breath, smile and look around at your audience. They will think that you are giving *them* time to think and to process what you have said previously. Only *you* will know that you are scrambling furiously in your brain trying to find your thought. Typically in less than five seconds you'll be back on track. If you're *still* blank, say: "Before we go any further does anyone have any questions?" That will buy you a little bit more time.

> Every time I close the door on reality
> it comes in through the window!
> Jennifer Unlimited

J. Projecting Your Charm And Charisma In Sales Situations And Interviews.

Good eye contact starts the minute you meet a client, a potential client, an interviewer or an audience.

You look him, her, or them in the eye, shake hands firmly, (No wimpy handshakes.) and say something personal and warm. "I've been looking forward to seeing you again." (Or meeting you). Keep looking directly into those eyes as you say those words. It projects honesty and sincerity.

When you walk into the interviewer's or prospect's office, walk briskly, shoulders back, head up and *smile!* As you enter the office, look around and try (perhaps desperately.) to find some clue as to the interests of the interviewer or prospect so you can start a conversation; preferably about something you have in common: A photo, an award, or a decoration. Hopefully, that item leads to a comment or question to elicit a "me-too" response.

- "Your children? How old are they? We have two boys, too!"
- "I see you received an award from Rotary. Have you been a member long? Nothing seems to go on in our town without the rotary."
- "What an unusual painting! Did you select it?"

As you sit down, mirror their body and the pace of their speech. *With any luck, your opening question or comment will launch a little small talk that will give you both a moment to get comfortable with each other.* However, don't linger on the small talk unless the interviewer or prospect initiates more small talk.

The rule: No more than 20% of the allotted appointment should be spent in small talk. A 20-minute appointment means you typically keep the small talk down to about 4 minutes. Some prospects/customers want to spend *most* of the time in small talk because getting to know you is far more important to them than getting to know your product. This is true for the personality profile known as "amiable" and it is also prevalent in the south and in rural areas. You'll have to trust your instincts here. If they want to get right down to business, do it. If they want to schmooze, schmooze.

I've had clients who would never let me get down to business. Then, all of a sudden, they'd say something like: "Can you get me a _____ by next Thursday?" And we didn't even discuss price!

The Real Secret To Charisma In Business And In Life Is . . .

🗝 To find everything - *people, events and things* - fascinating.

🗝 To be so well prepared that you ooooooooze confidence and assurance.

🗝 To be outwardly focused.

🗝 To be observant.

🗝 To enjoy yourself and let others do the same.

Maybe you cannot fully master all of these skills immediately, but if you make just a little headway in each area you will be closer to being charismatic. *Now, wasn't that fun?*

Linda Brakeall and Anna Wildermuth

Just for you . . .

What three things are you going to do to unlock your charisma?

1.

2.

3.

What must you STOP doing in order to project charm and charisma?

What inspirations or insights did you get from this chapter?

What else do you need to know? We might be able to help. Email us. ann@personalimagesinc.com
      Linda@LindaBrakeall.com

> If you can't be a good example,
> then you'll just have to be
> a horrible warning.
> **Catherine Aird**

> The possibility of stepping into a higher plane
> is quite real for everyone.
> It requires no force or sacrifice.
> It involves little more than changing
> our ideas about what is normal.
> **Deepak Chopra**

Unlocking The Secrets of Successful Women in Business

Key 5

Your Personal Style!

Discover, Develop And Define Your Own Personal Style.

When your personal and professional style is authentic you, and everyone around you, feels comfortable.

Clues About Your Personal Style:

🔑 You may like the formality, or the finished look of always wearing a jacket, sweater, shawl, scarf or a "third piece."

🔑 You may "live" in pants/slacks.

🔑 Almost all of your suits have skirts or almost all have pants.

🔑 Perhaps you favor high contrast colors (black, white and red) or a monochrome palette (brown, beige and cream).

🗝 Maybe you "live" in only *your* colors and/or fabrics that make you feel good.

🗝 Everything you wear may come from LL Bean. (Or from Frederick's of Hollywood. Please, *please* tell me you shop elsewhere for business clothes!)

🗝 Maybe you choose to have only a few good pieces of jewelry that you wear most of the time – or you have specific jewelry for specific outfits. You could wear only antique jewelry – or no jewelry. Perhaps you wear only cloisonné, or all gold, or all silver.

🗝 You may prefer a very tailored look – or a softer, more feminine look.

🗝 Maybe you never leave your house without full makeup – or makeup is only for special occasions.

When others see you they are gathering impressions of all the pieces that outwardly represent your style.

In one glance, they have observed your hair, skin and makeup, your clothing, shoes and accessories, your grooming, your body language and your "presence."

They notice if your clothes fit correctly and are appropriate for the occasion. They react positively or negatively to the colors you have chosen for your hair and clothing. That all contributes to your own personal or professional style.

The authors' intent is not to dictate your style, merely to encourage you to consider new choices and opportunities as you re-think and refine your external image. Notice celebrities' and politicians' clothes and the way they conduct themselves. Those things enhance who they are. You may admire the fact that they are consistent or inconsistent in their appearance. (Or maybe consistent in their inconsistency . . .like Madonna, or Hillary Clinton in the 90's?)

Unlocking The Secrets of Successful Women in Business

In the business world consistency indicates reliability.

The key is to appear current and appropriate for your profession because what works for the senior level bank executive does not necessarily work for the ad agency executive. Think carefully about the image you choose to convey.

Find someone to identify with.

Look at your peers and celebrity role models. Is there one with a similar body type and coloring?

Collect pictures of this person. And then do a spreadsheet. List what you like about her image, clothing, colors, makeup, hair and style. Note what she wore on different occasions and why you like the look. Why does it work for her? Would it be appropriate for you professionally? This is the time to be coldly analytical.

Fill this in to compare.

YOU	ROLE MODEL
Height	Height
Body type	Body type
Weight	Guess weight
Size	Guess size
Eyes	Eyes
Skin tone	Skin tone
Hair color	Hair color
Favorite color	Favorite color
Favorite outfit	Favorite outfit

🔑 How would you describe her style?

🔑 Are there enough similarities for her to be your role model?

🔑 Would her style work for you? If not, could it be modified to work for you?

🔑 If you are going to closely emulate her style, what do you need to buy, adapt, or eliminate?

Use a personal shopper.

Here's good news: You don't have to do it alone. Go to one of the better department stores in town. They have personal shoppers who will work with you one-on-one at no extra cost to you. In fact, they often *save you money* because they know what will work in your profession, on your body and with your coloring. She might also nudge you in the right direction for hairstyle and color. You will make far fewer buying mistakes and if time is a challenge, as it is for most of us, a personal shopper can save you time too.

After working a few times with a personal shopper that you trust, you can call ahead and say, "Pat, I need a new suit for an important presentation with bankers. (Or a country club casual conference, or a gala.) Can you find something for me? Accessories, shoes and all? I'll stop by tomorrow afternoon if you're free." You walk in. She has four outfits. You choose one or two. And you're done!

A friend, Rita Emmett, was all set to start her publicity tour for her new book, The Procrastinator's Handbook. Her publisher brought her to New York and promptly sent her to Bloomingdale's to work with a personal shopper for her TV interviews. The personal shopper said when they met, "Rita, you may or may not buy clothing today, but when you leave here, *you will know* what colors and styles will work for you on television." Rita said in less than an hour, she had a whole new way of looking at her professional wardrobe. You can do that, too. Even if you're not going to be on TV.

Four Personal Styles

Sophisticated, **stylish and classic** looks established, timeless and every detail is precise such as this sheath with jacket, and executive suit. Madelyn Albright, Jacqueline Kennedy Onassis, Barbara Walters and Liz Vargus, are all good and very different examples of this style

Feminine **usually showcases the figure**. First Lady Laura Bush personifies the feminine style as does former presidential hopeful, Elizabeth Dole. Clothes are closer to the body with softer lines and softer colors. The flared skirt and Chanel style jacket below are soft, easy fitting and feminine.

Dramatic makes a statement. It is very fashion motivated and often high contrast. A black cashmere shawl artfully draped is dramatic as is this shawl-collared wrap jacket. When you think dramatic, think about Cher, Venus Williams, and Madonna. There are undoubtedly some dramatic businesswomen, but none who have captured the public attention.

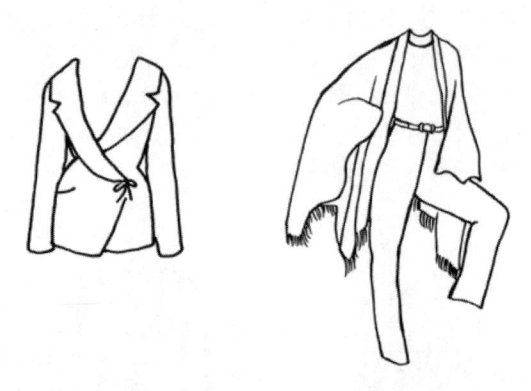

Sporty is a natural, very casual look influenced by fitness and the outdoors. A sporty business casual look might be a polo shirt or a turtleneck under a short jacket over slacks. The sporty look is a personal style of Candice Bergman and Katie Couric.

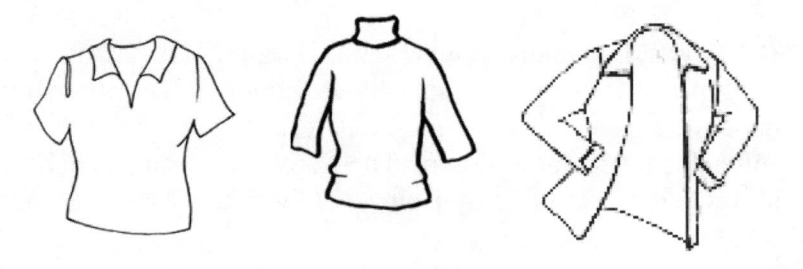

> I base most of my "style"
> on what doesn't itch!
> Gildna Radner

Look timeless!

Whatever your personal style, profession and age, keep your look current. If you wore it in college, and that was more than five years ago, you probably need an updated look.

Many women are in professions or companies where they are younger or older than those around them. It is tempting to try to fit in and wear "what *they* wear." *Resist the impulse.* Keep the following ideas in mind, and notice how similar they are. The goal is to look timeless and current, not trendy.

To look older:

Let your knowledge and hard work send the message that you are more mature than your years. Avoid clothes that are too-anything; too short, too tight, too much skin, too young, or too matronly. Get rid of hair that is too long, too curly, or severe. Buy classic, simple jewelry rather than "fun" jewelry for the office. Get a simple, classic watch and good-looking pen. Consider eyeglasses as a prop for those times when you really want to look serious.

To look younger:

Think clean-cut, streamlined and classic. Avoid clutter and clothes that are too-anything; too short, too long, too tight, too much skin, too trendy. Get rid of hair that is too long, too curly, or severe. Choose clothing and make-up colors that give your skin a vibrant, healthy glow.

> Change is inevitable.
> Growth is optional.
> Anonymous

4 Keys To Successful Personal Style

1. Clothes fits your lifestyle.
2. Clothes are comfortable.
3. Clothing that is classic and current.
4. Clothes and jewelry that is appropriate for the occasion and "feels like you."

Just For You . . .

List 3 action steps to take to make your personal style consistent.

1.

2.

3.

What must you STOP doing in order to create a consistent personal style?

What inspirations or insights did you get from this chapter?

> To follow without halt, one aim;
> there is the secret of success.
> And success? What is it?
> I do not find it in the applause of the theater.
> It lies rather in the satisfaction of accomplishment.
> Anna Pavlova

Key 6

Professional Style

Your Professional Style Is Based On Your Personal Style.

A style that consistently fits your personality and your career is a combination of your clothing style, color choices and how you combine and wear clothes. Have you ever gone shopping with a friend who found something and said, "This is you!" *That* is your signature style. Just be sure it is the "image" that you want to project.

Example: My (Anna's) style is classic. I wear clothes that are simple in design and most of the time in solid colors with uncluttered jewelry. As an image consultant, I know it is important not to intimidate others and my clothes must set the tone for the work I do. I want to look smart and stylish but I can't be a fashion setter.

The authors' "business uniform" as consultants, trainers and speakers is a solid color suit with a silky blouse and a power accent such as a substantial pin, or a scarf. Add earrings, a good watch, coordinated hose and 2-inch pumps and we're ready to walk out the door. Of course, that's not what we wear *all* the time, but that is our first thought which we modify for the occasion.

> *Create your own "business uniform"*
> *that is comfortable, stylish,*
> *and appropriate for your industry.*

Subtly mirror your female boss or other women in authority in your field. If you dress in the manner she does, she will tend to think you are like her; thus wonderful. Don't buy identical clothes and accessories; instead understand what her "uniform" conveys. Work towards sending a similar, but not competing, message if you want to follow in her footsteps. Her uniform may say:

- I'm the boss!
- Love me.
- Trust me.
- I'm stylish.
- I'm competent.

A Signature Style Defines Who You Are Professionally.

It gives others a glimpse of where you are on the corporate ladder...or *if* you are on the corporate ladder. Here are three basic professional styles for you to consider and combine with your own personal style.

Unlocking The Secrets of Successful Women in Business

1. The Chairman Of The Board:

(We know that "Chairman" is not politically correct, but the other choices don't send the same message.) If you are a corporate senior level executive — VP to CEO — (or if you plan to be one in the foreseeable future) in any industry, your professional style is classic and powerful.

Your "look" needs to say:

- I know who I am.
- I have authority and power!
- The buck stops here.
- Traditional in most cases.
- Proficient and savvy.

**We are what we repeatedly do.
Aristotle**

Linda Brakeall and Anna Wildermuth

The "Chairman Of The Board" wears:

🗝 Suits and dresses in the highest quality fabrics and design in solids, small, subtle patterns and classic darker colors, or muted tones of navy, black, burgundy and gray. Sling backs add a feminine touch to a "power suit."

🗝 A "power accent" such as a pin, or a contrasting scarf, such as a red scarf with a navy suit. (Men use ties as power accents.)

🗝 Genuine gold or silver jewelry.

🗝 High quality shoes, handbags and briefcase.

🗝 Classic watch and pen

"Problems are good, not bad.
Welcome them and become the solution.
When you have solved enough problems,
people will thank you."
Mark Victor Hansen

2. The Communicator:

If you are an account rep, teacher, trainer, facilitator, speaker, in human resources, customer service, a salesperson in any field, or a consultant your professional style is warm and trustworthy.

Your "look" needs to say:

- I'm genuine, accessible and honest.
- I'm knowledgeable.
- I can help you.
- I'm approachable and reliable.

The communicator wears:

- Matching or compatible jackets over dresses, skirts, slacks and sweater sets in medium-range colors.
- Soft fabrics in solids or small, subtle prints.
- Simple, classic jewelry.
- Mid-priced shoes, handbags and briefcase.

3. The Artist:

If you are in advertising, arts, fashion, or you are a personality, author or entertainer, your professional style is dramatic and high fashion.

Your "look" needs to say:

- 🔑 I'm creative, on the cutting edge, one of a kind
- 🔑 Look at me!
- 🔑 I'm dramatic!
- 🔑 I'm confident.

The artist wears:

- 🔑 The "new look" first
- 🔑 Larger, more definite accessories to project confidence.
- 🔑 Sometimes trendy and "fashion forward" ensembles, but does not mix fashion styles.
- 🔑 Adventurous apparel in brighter colors but avoids looking cheap in the pursuit of looking trendy.

No Need To Follow All The Rules All The Time!

No matter your field, profession, personal or professional style, sometimes you just want to look different, but who has time to shop? Change the look and change the message with accessories. Let's demonstrate this concept by starting with a basic dark suit.

Make it dramatic!
Accent with a brightly colored, high-contrast, scarf or blouse to make it dramatic. Large, bold, unusual pieces of jewelry are dramatic, as are designer shoes.

Make it classic!
Accent with a cream or taupe blouse or scarf, and simple gold or silver jewelry.

Make it feminine!
Accent with a soft print blouse or pastel sweater, and pearl earrings and pin or necklace.

To Create Your Own Professional Signature Style That Sends The Message You Intend, You Must Understand That Your Image Is An Equation.

Equation Examples:
Anna is tall, thin, and reserved. She can wear dramatic, outrageous, or even very soft ensembles and still be taken seriously because she is dark haired and her personality and demeanor announces that she is a serious person. She chooses to project a very professional, tailored image. Anna's challenge is to look

warmer and friendlier so she often lightens up the image with lighter colors.

For Linda, who smiles all the time, the challenge is to project an image that encourages people to listen to the substance of what she says and not be side-tracked by the high energy and enthusiastic personality. Linda dresses in a very tailored manner, in darker, serious colors, so people will understand the whole package.

You, too, are an equation. What needs to be emphasized? What needs to be played down? Think about your physical attributes as well as your coloring and personality.

Accessories often define your style.
Here are a few tips from e-how.com.

Accessorize your work wardrobe.

– Choose shoes, jewelry, watches and belts from such classic materials as leather, silver and gold.

– Individualize yourself. Suits and pantsuits are traditional office wear for women, but you can spice them up with a personal trademark. A slim silver bangle, small hoop earrings or a silver hair clip can be elegant additions to your black pantsuit.

– Select an unobtrusive watch that goes with a variety of outfits. Ideally, it should have simple lines and a neutral band.

– Wear classic jewelry. A pearl necklace, diamond studs, jade bangles or small beads add an air of sophistication.

– Make sure the metal of your accessories matches: keep it all silver or all gold.

– Clip your hair up using leather, metal or shell clips and bands. They will keep your hair neat as well as adding style.

– Wear neutral panty hose or socks.

– Make sure your shoes match your bag. Brown, black, gray and tan palettes dress up everything. Leather shoes are still classic, but high-tech micro fibers

Unlocking The Secrets of Successful Women in Business

look and wear great, too. A touch of fun in your shoes, such as a big buckle or a funky heel, can be stylish and not over-the-top.

– Stick to low heels and classic shoes for comfort and an understated look.

– Observe what your colleagues are wearing. Follow the spirit, but don't be intimidated by it.

– Your nails and hair color are accessories, too. Choose according to the work environment.

Reprinted with permission from www.ehow.com.

5 Keys To Successful Professional Style:

1. Dress to reflect your professional status
2. Define your style with clothing, accessories and color.
3. Create a business uniform for specific occasions such as sales calls and presentations.
4. Seamlessly blend your personal and professional styles.

Thank goodness I was never sent to school;
it would have rubbed off some of the originality.
Beatrix Potter

Just for you . . .

List 3 action steps to put your professional style in place:

1.

2.

3.

What do you need to STOP doing in order to seamlessly blend your personal and professional styles?

What inspirations or insights did you get from this chapter?

What else do you need to know? We might be able to help.
Email us.   anna@personalimagesinc.com
　　　　　　Linda@LindaBrakeall.com

**Who ever thought up the word "mammogram?"
Every time I hear it, I think I'm supposed to put
my breasts in an envelope and send them to someone!
Jan King**

Unlocking The Secrets of Successful Women in Business
Key 7

Secrets Of Business Casual

Professional women are constantly challenged in the area of business-casual dressing. The key is to have a business-like presence that is neither too formal nor too casual because either extreme gives away authority. Of course, you want to look like you're a team member. Simultaneously, it is important that your image sends the message, "leader," even — or *especially* — if the world is not yet aware that you *are* a leader.

I've lately come to the conclusion that it's actually *easier* for women than men to project an appropriate air of business casual. "Appropriate" is the important word here. Pantsuits are automatically more casual than skirted suits, and with a soft sweater, or casual blouse your look is both casual and business-like. You'll convey authority, but you won't look up-tight.

Linda Brakeall and Anna Wildermuth

Does Biz-Caz Affect Productivity?

It depends upon the field, the corporate culture and the individuals. We wish there was a simpler, easier, one-size-fits-all answer, but there's not. The Silicon Valley, dot com companies and many places where there are no clocks *and no customers* perform better with no dress codes whatsoever. Try to put those creative, march-to-their-own-drummer mavericks into anything that remotely resembles a corporate uniform and you're looking for trouble.

But that is not who this book is for. This book is for the woman who wants to make a difference in the business world, who interacts with customers and other businesses. She may be climbing the corporate ladder, making sales calls, in human resources, training, or marketing. She wants to be noticed for the right things, she wants to get ahead, and she knows that the folks who frequent the boardroom still wear suits or the equivalent.

Appropriate business casual.

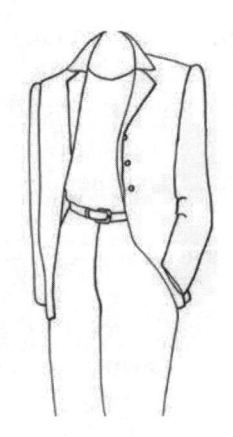

In the kind of company *she* works in, too-casual does affect productivity, and usually not in an upward direction. If she travels abroad for business, business casual will encourage the idea that women can't be taken seriously. It will be harder for her to get the job done efficiently. Clothes that **do not qualify** as professional business casual include anything that you might *consider* wearing to the beach, running in the park, cleaning the garage, gardening, mowing the lawn or working out.

> **Too often women born after the mid-sixties have spent the bulk of their professional lives in "biz-caz." They feel "funny" in suits.
> Get over it!**

Perhaps you will have to regard professional apparel as costuming. If so, *Happy Halloween!* You need to get into the habit of dressing better *now,* so that you'll be comfortable when the stakes are high. You can't wait until you have a meeting with "important" folks to drag out the "grown up clothes." You'll feel as uncomfortable and self-conscious as you would in a southern belle ball-gown! That uncomfortable feeling will be reflected in everything that you say and do and you will have a very hard time being your usual, charming, knowledgeable self.

If you are strictly in a dot com world and *only* work with other Gen Xer's and Nexters, as co-workers, clients and customers, you may get away with it. However, the usual business scenario involves customers and clients who may expect more than jeans, khaki's and polo shirts. Those people may not take you seriously. If you are offending the people who have money to buy your product or services, perhaps you might want to rethink your business wardrobe.

When you're deciding what to wear to the office, you might ask yourself this question: *How would I feel if I ran into my most important client dressed like this*? If the answer is anything less than *"Great!"* change clothes before you go to work.

> Your "image" is content visible.
> It tells the world who you are.
> Anna Wildermuth

Linda Brakeall and Anna Wildermuth

Business Casual Rules For Women Executives And Will-Be Executives:

🔑 **Suits earn respect**. A suit can be dressed down with an open neck shirt or a soft sweater and still give you a finished, professional look.

🔑 **Matching or compatible jackets** convey executive presence and authority.

🔑 **Darker colors convey power;** lighter colors are more casual in appearance.

🔑 **Add simple, understated jewelry** such as a necklace or pin to business casual apparel to add authority without intimidation.

🔑 **Dressing casually does not mean giving up quality clothes**; it means the opposite. Casual clothes must be the best quality and be very well maintained because it is much harder to look professional and command respect when casually dressed.

🔑 **Simple cuts** always work well in clothing. Full linings, better buttons and topstitching add quality.

🔑 **Relaxed clothing choices include** softer fabrics such as knits in wool and cotton, sweater sets, pants suits, jackets with softer shoulders.

🔑 **Weekend casual is *not* business casual.**

Unlocking The Secrets of Successful Women in Business

Business Casual:
Is Your Company Losing Money?
Guest columnist Dawn E. Waldrop

You walk into a company and the first words are, "Please excuse our office - it's dress down day." Stop - stop right now. If casual dress was working no one would be apologizing or even saying anything.

Can business casual work if done appropriately? Yes, however most people do not know what casual attire is for the office. Why? First of all this is a learned skill we are not taught in school. How many of you have ever taken a course for a whole semester on professional dress? None, because there is no such course. Someday there will be.

If no one taught you how to do your job what would happen? You would muddle through. Umm, interesting, because that is exactly what most people do when they stand in front of their closet each morning.

People do not intentionally dress inappropriately. It is because they do not know what to do. Employees need to be taught **how** just as they are taught how to do their job. **Stop** trying to bring in casual dress. Instead **teach** company people the three levels of dress: power professional, professional and business casual. Then **let them choose** how they want to be perceived.

How much money is the company losing? How much more money could the company be making were all employees presenting themselves professionally at all times? How much more money could you be making? Dressing professionally never works against you. Dressing unprofessionally does.

Think about how you feel when you walk into a medical facility and cannot figure out who the nurse, doctor or patient is -- because they all look alike. We cannot tell the difference between the corporate executive and the office visitor. We cannot tell the difference between the customer and the sales clerk in the stores.

To clients, there is a comfort in immediately recognizing the professional. Attire is that powerful communication tool. Here are three tips for dressing business casual.

First: Keep the business casual wardrobe a separate wardrobe. By keeping it a separate wardrobe the mind will be on the job. If clothes are worn on the weekend and then to work the mind is still on the weekend.

Second: Clothes will stay neater and professional. Let's face it; on the weekend we are not paying attention to keeping our clothes clean. By keeping business casual a separate wardrobe you never have to worry about wearing something to work to find it has a stain or tear.

Third: You will save money. If an outfit starts to get worn but still has some more wearing left, then move it to the weekend attire.

If you are one of those people who do not feel comfortable in business casual here are tips to be more casual yet highly professional.

> Women: Wear a sweater top in place of a silk blouse.
>
> Men: Wear a medium to dark colored shirt in place of a white or light colored shirt.
>
> Women: Wear a flat professional shoe, accessorize and wear basic make up. As soon as women wear pants they become business casual. Wear a trouser style pants or pant suit.

Give serious consideration to how you want others to perceive you and the company. As human beings we get different energies from clothes. You feel different in a suit compared to a casual outfit. When you feel the difference so do the people around you.

Ask yourself this question before you leave for work everyday, "If a client or guest walked in the office today do I feel **totally** professional in what I am wearing?" If everyone in the company cannot answer "yes" then your company is most likely losing money.

By Dawn E. Waldrop, image expert and national speaker, can be contacted at 440.572.1890 or web site: www.best-impressions.com.

**Do the best you can in every task,
no matter how unimportant it may seem at the time.
No one learns more about a problem
than the person at the bottom.
Sandra Day O'Connor**

Unlocking The Secrets of Successful Women in Business

5 Keys To Successful Business Casual:

1. Outfits must be suitable for meeting clients/customers.
2. Choose compatible jackets with skirts or slacks for a finished casual look.
3. All clothes must fit well and be in perfect condition.
4. Monochromatic suits in lighter (but not pastel) colors definitely say "business" but look more casual.
5. Add soft sweaters to suits to relax the look.

**The greater danger for most of us is not
that our aim is too high and we miss it,
but that it is too low and we reach it.
Michelangelo**

Just for you . . .

List 3 action steps to update your business casual wardrobe.

1.

2.

3.

What do you need to STOP doing in order to project an aura of *business* in your business casual clothes?

What inspirations or insights did you get from this chapter?

Linda Brakeall and Anna Wildermuth
Key 8

Approachability!

A Sincere, Relaxed Smile Is The Key To Approachability.

Webster's dictionary defines "approachability" as capable of being approached, accessible, easy to meet and deal with. Doing business today is all about whom you know and who knows you. Is it easy to get to know you? If you answer, "yes" to these three questions, you're probably approachable.

- 🔑 Do people often and easily smile at you?
- 🔑 Do people introduce themselves to you?
- 🔑 In meetings, do people share ideas easily with you?

> Loves conquers all things except poverty and toothaches.
> Mae West

Unlocking The Secrets of Successful Women in Business

Approachability, Ethnicity, Diversity and Color.

If you are African American, Hispanic, Native American, Asian, Martian, or anything else that might possibly be termed "different," the key is to understand how certain colors and styles will be perceived in your profession and how careful selection of clothing can help you blend in, stand out, appear approachable or aloof.

As a professional woman, it's not appropriate to wear ethnicity on your sleeve. Your ethnicity is who you are, but it is not *all* that you are. We all want to be accepted for our merits, our talents, our experiences, our personalities and the "whole package," not merely because of our heritage. And we want people to feel comfortable enough to talk to us and get to know us. Not to avoid us just because we seem or look "different."

Karen Lucas who is a tall, elegant, very striking, African-American, makes being "different" work for her by turning it into a major asset. She has found her own style of dressing and communicating that is always approachable and never intimidating. Karen says:

> " I am a full partner in a management consulting firm providing coaching and consultative expertise to senior level executives in multiple industries. When presenting my credentials, along with my partners, to prospective clients, I am cognizant at all times of a significant fact. I AM, MORE OFTEN THAN NOT, PERCEIVED AS DIFFERENT. The eloquence of my speech, the professional impact of my appearance, is secondary to my being seen not first as a valued resource, but a valued Black resource."

It's true that some people won't like you because you are "different." They may have opinions about you based upon *nothing that you did or said.* Remember that other people's opinions are only their *opinions*. That doesn't make it so. (If someone called you a teapot, would you be a teapot? That's only an opinion. Or poor vision!)

If you find individuals "turning you off" or "tuning you out" before they know you well enough to do so with reason, consider that it may merely be lack of knowledge of your "type." Don't take it personally, because we all tend to like people who are like ourselves. Maintain your professional presence and stay open and friendly. Given time, they often warm up.

Your Own Personal Palette Of Hair, Skin, Eyes, And Physical Build Often Determine, At Least To Some Extent, Other People's Comfort With You.

It often has to do with the people they grew up with. Linda's sons are invariably attracted to fair-skinned and fair-haired women since boys usually fall in love with women like their mothers. Anna's son finds dark, exotic women far more appealing. A lot of it is simply familiarity.

Make your personal palette work for you by choosing a professional palette of clothing colors and styles that provide balance.

Blondes, especially the softer, natural looking blondes are usually viewed as very approachable. However, they are often not taken very seriously. A tailored look in medium colors would permit them to be both approachable and business-like. Goldie Hawn, blonde and giggly, usually looks like a lightweight, but she's had several serious roles. With tailored outfits, and without the giggle, she was believable as an executive.

Very tall or heavy people can be intimidating. Wear medium solid colors rather than unrelieved dark colors to appear more open and approachable. With darker colors, add some color around the face, and *smile!* Al Gore, a big man with dark hair and a serious demeanor, in the 2000 election opted for earth tones to "lighten up" his image.

A dark haired person with dark skin color becomes more approachable by wearing clothes in neutral and pale colors. Even very dark women can wear flattering, subtle colors with the proper makeup. We've seen several TV news-anchors pull off this combination effectively.

Extremely attractive people often seem to be unapproachable. Would you walk up to David Copperfield in his black leather jacket? Careful clothing choices can permit you to be attractive without intimidation. Save the dramatic, fashion-plate look for social occasions.

These famous people always seem very approachable.

If you happened to see these people at a party and they weren't otherwise engaged, you might walk up and say "Hi!"

- Katie Couric. Great smile, pixie hair, boundless enthusiasm.
- Oprah Winfrey. Great smile, warm eyes, good listener, easy body language.
- Barbara Bush. Great smile, trademark costume-jewelry pearls, soft, white hair and sparkling eyes.
- Mary Lou Retton. Unstoppable smile and high energy.

One might be reluctant to start an uninvited conversation with these people.

🗝 Princess Margaret. Stiff body language and hair, forced smile, matronly and regal attire.

🗝 Hillary Clinton. Very polished suits and stiff hair, forced smile, stiff body language.

🗝 Joan Collins. Dark hair, dramatic fashions, cold eyes, heavy make-up.

5 Keys To Approachability:

1. Smile!
2. Maintain easy body language – stay away from stiff folded hands.
3. Choose clothing and colors to balance your business style.
4. Engage people with sincere eye contact.
5. Introduce yourself first.

*The true worth of a race
must be measured by the character of its womanhood.*
Mary McLeod Bethune

*The trouble with the rat race
is that even if you win, you're still a rat.*
Lily Tomlin

Unlocking The Secrets of Successful Women in Business

Just for you . . .

List 3 action steps to become more approachable.

1.

2.

3.

What do you need to STOP doing in order to become more approachable?

What inspirations or insights did you get from this chapter?

What else do you need to know? We might be able to help.
Email us. anna@personalimagesinc.com
           Linda@LindaBrakeall.com

>The most beautiful things in the world
>cannot be seen, or touched...
>but are felt within the heart.
>Helen Keller

>If we are to achieve a richer culture,
>rich in contrasting values,
>we must recognize the whole gamut
>of human potentialities.
>We must weave a social fabric in which
>each diverse human gift will find a fitting place.
>Margaret Mead

Linda Brakeall and Anna Wildermuth

Key 9

Color Codes

Each Industry And Level Of Business Has Designated Colors That Project Messages And Emotions.

You need to understand the rules to play the game. The following examples are certainly not the only colors used, and these are not the only colors you can wear in these industries, merely the ones that are the most widely accepted as "in" and comfortable for that industry. Power colors are darker or muted.

- Blues, grays, and maybe maroon in corporate America, finance, law, or a service business.
- Browns, dark greens and teal blues in health care.
- Deep plums, rust and unique trims in art, advertising.

Unlocking The Secrets of Successful Women in Business

🔑 In general, avoid black anytime you are trying to persuade or sell.

🔑 High contrast sends a power message; monochrome is more approachable.

How Important Is Color Professionally?

When you see a woman, the first thing you notice is the color she's wearing, then you notice the outfit, then you notice the fit. Color says a lot about how you view yourself, how you're feeling, and it has an impact on others around you. Don't you feel a wee bit happier when you wear or see someone in red or sunshine yellow? Do you just assume a person wearing red or yellow is "perky?" Or do you think that she just wants to make a statement, or get attention?

Color has its own language and sends messages to those around you. Use it effectively based on your own physical coloring and the relationship of a specific color to your profession and industry.

Color Capsules

Color capsules are the basis of every wardrobe. Each color capsule should have three colors, two dominants and one accent. The accent color can be used as your signature color. Two or three color capsules will give you a lot of variety and with careful planning some of the pieces can be worn with more than one capsule.

Usually there are two or three medium to dark dominant colors that you build your wardrobe around and a savvy trick is to have an accent color or two that will work with all of your dominant colors.

Consistently use two to three dominant colors in your wardrobe. Buying and coordinating a wardrobe will be easier and give you a smart "look."

Examples: As a classic *Winter*, I, (Anna) might use black, gray and plum for dominant colors and choose a few jewel tones for accents. Or choose to soften my look with browns and beiges as dominant colors with accent of gold and cream.

Autumn Linda's dominant colors are teal, navy and brown. They can all be accented with various shades of gold, yellow and aqua to compliment Linda's red hair, blue eyes and fair skin. Rhonda Fleming, beautiful redheaded movie star from another era, suggested that savvy redheads work with only one dominant and one accent color and count the red hair as the other dominant color for each outfit.

Signature Color

Having a signature color, usually an accent color, sends a message about how you view yourself. This is the color you are personally drawn to and if you look in your closet you'll find it frequently. As an accent, you can wear it most of the time. Nancy Reagan's signature color was red and we saw her in red dresses and red Adolpho suits. Since red is a strong color, it works for main pieces like suits but may be intimidating. However, for a petite First Lady, that wasn't an issue.

> If you're not feeling good about you, what you're wearing outside doesn't mean a thing.
> Leontyne Price

Exercise caution when you wear your signature color in your main pieces because color influences the way others perceive you.

Example: A pink accent in a blouse or a scarf is a softening influence. A pink suit is too soft to display authority unless you're Mary Kay Ash and own your own successful corporation.

You might want to read books about color like <u>Color Me Beautiful,</u> <u>Rainbow In Your Eye, Color Me A Season,</u> <u>Women Of Color,</u> or visit a good department store and find a color specialist who can tell you quickly the colors that are both flattering and appropriate for your industry.

To do it yourself, gather up lots of color swatches, pieces of fabric, colored scarves, blouses in medium to darker/muted colors for suits and dresses and find lighter colors for blouses and scarves.

Put on your regular makeup. Look into a mirror in bright natural light as you hold a color up to your face. Does it make your skin look clearer and warmer? Do your eyes sparkle? Do you feel good in this color? If so, this is one of *your* colors!

When you discover your signature color, you'll look "Maahvellous, dahling! Simply maahvellous!"

Linda Brakeall and Anna Wildermuth

The Often-Discussed Season-Colors Should Be Used As Guidelines, Not As Absolutes In Determining The Colors You Wear.

A few years ago the rules were firmly written in wide tip, permanent magic markers. Only "Winters" wore jewel tones. Only "Summers" wore pastels. "Autumns" wore vibrant "nature" colors and "Springs" wore the softer hues of those colors. All that has changed. With the proper make-up and the right accent colors, most of us can wear some shade of almost any color that is appropriate for the occasion, your profession and industry.

If certain colors are almost "required" for your industry but are not usually flattering to you, you may be able to change the accent color to make it work.

I (Anna) always avoided browns until it occurred to me to accent them with taupe and gold. Even a Winter like me can wear brown with those accents. Linda works with a lot of bankers who *live* in navy. Linda, a typical Autumn stayed away from navy blue for years because it "washed her out" and made her look like a sickly heroine from a Jane Austen novel. While navy will never be her very own favorite color, she's found that if she wears a yellow or aqua blouse, the navy no longer makes her look faded and tired. Got the idea?

Following are some examples of famous people you may know and their "season." Perhaps you can find one whose coloring resembles yours to get an idea for colors that will suit you best. Winters and Summers have a cool blue tint to their skin and the Autumns and Springs have a warm golden hue.

Unlocking The Secrets of Successful Women in Business

Famous Autumns
(Subtle golden skin tint, slightly more vivid coloring than Springs.)

Emma Thomson, actress
Julia Roberts, actress
Linda Brakeall, author, speaker
Katie Couric, TV news anchor
Venus Williams, tennis star

Famous Springs
(Subtle golden skin tint.)

Meg Ryan, actress
Goldie Hawn, actress
Marilyn Monroe, actress
Glenn Close, actress
Betsy Holden, CEO of Kraft foods

Famous Winters
(Subtle bluish skin tint, slightly more vivid coloring than Summers.)

Elizabeth Taylor, actress
Anna Wildermuth, author, image consultant
Cher, entertainer
Oprah Winfrey, TV personality, entrepreneur
Andrea Jung, CEO of Avon

Famous Summers
(Subtle bluish skin tint.)

Princess Grace
Diane Sawyer, TV news anchor
Hillary Clinton, politician
Gwyneth Paltrow, actress
Jane Clayton, TV news anchor

Linda Brakeall and Anna Wildermuth

The Psychology And Symbolic Language Of Color

Black: Black intimidates others and can drain color from your face. The new blue-black is elegant and sophisticated for the evening, but solid black is seldom flattering without an accent color to enhance your coloring.

Blue: Lighter shades of blue represent serenity and peace while the darker shades, like the blue-black navy, represent authority, respect, stability and business.

Blue-Green: Teals, dark blue greens and hunter greens are now worn in business. Blue and grayed tones project power, while the greener tones signal casual wear and approachability.

Brown: Brown has become very popular due to the business casual atmosphere in corporate America. Combined with grays and blues, it has gained an authority image without being intimating. However, this is *not* the color for a board meeting or a formal presentation because it does not send a "power" message."

Burgundy: Upscale burgundy is a more sophisticated, traditional red with a royal air to it. Red-burgundy is easier to wear for most women than blue-burgundy.

Gray: With so many shades of gray, most people can find a shade that will work. Darker grays have more authority than lighter.

Green: Green is approachable and the darkest shades have authority. Olives and greens found in nature work well for business casual.

Orange: Orange is often used in sports clothing. It is considered fun and periodically very high fashion. I (Anna) do not recommend orange for corporate business wear unless you are

Unlocking The Secrets of Successful Women in Business

in the fashion industry. It can be can be toned down with browns and grays for everyday wear in some industries but orange has no power or authority.

Red: It is a very aggressive color and debate continues about the propriety of women in red in business. Burgundy and deep red plums are more sophisticated versions of red and are considered good colors for a senior level image.

Yellow: Yellow is a color for fun and shock value. Great for athletic wear and high fashion. Not appropriate for corporate suits but it makes a cheerful accent color.

White: White will add crispness to black. There are many shades of white, from warm ivory-cream to flat chalk-white. Most people can wear some shade of white.

For more on this topic read, Power Of Color by Dr. Morton Walker and Color Psychology by Angela Wright.

> From birth to age eighteen, a girl needs good parents.
> From eighteen to thirty-five, she needs good looks.
> From thirty-five to fifty-five,
> she needs a good personality.
> From fifty-five on, she needs good cash.
> Sophie Tucker

Linda Brakeall and Anna Wildermuth

The Energy Of Color And Fashion Feng Shui
Guest Columnist Denise Butchko

Color is as much a part of our lives as television, floral bouquets and "closets filled with nothing to wear." We've transitioned from white diapers to colorful clothing without much thought or intention. Yet color can easily and effortlessly serve us in ways most of us have ignored.

You probably had a favorite color when you were growing up – and, in fact, there may still be a color you love the most. Or maybe you have certain colors or clothing items that you designate for "special occasions." (One client has her lucky shopping underwear.) Have you ever thought about why? Or what kind of energy it provides?

You have probably heard things like "red is a power color" or "blue makes people feel they can trust you." "purple has the highest spiritual vibration" and "black makes you look thinner." But why? What is it about color that draws people to these conclusions? And how can you make color work for – and not against – you?

Looking to nature sheds some light. One perspective of recent popularity incorporates the ancient Chinese art of feng shui. By utilizing the properties of the five life forming elements of water, wood, fire, earth and metal – you can match the energy of people and circumstances to make a better, quicker connection on an energetic level to work in your favor. And nature provides a dependable base from which to move forward. Correlations will make sense and associations will be easy to see.

Feng shui is based on the premise that individuals are energetically linked to their environments; and that their prosperity is enhanced by harmonious and balanced surroundings. So if you want to represent yourself authentically and create situations that work in your favor – try incorporating the following elements into the shape, color and substance of what you wear in order to create the energy you wish to manifest.

The water element is represented by wavy, free form shapes and the colors of dark blue and black. It has a sensual, exotic message. It is also considered a "deep" energy, often unconventional and relying on the intuitive.

The wood element is represented by columnar shapes and the colors of blue and green. It has an active, energizing message. It is also considered a very fun, rejuvenating and action-filled energy that likes to play and compete.

Angular, pointed shapes and hues represent the fire element from the red color family. It has an attractive, exciting message. It is also considered to be the dominant energy of the jet-setting, fashionable and theatrical crowd.

Square shapes and the colors of brown, orange and yellow represent the earth element. It has an essential, grounded message. It is also considered to be a very conservative, authentic and natural energy.

The metal element is represented by circles and ovals and by white, pastels and metallic. It has a refined, elegant message. It is also considered to a subtle, feminine, reserved energy.

So – in order to make colors work for you – one scenario could be: You are going on job interview to a bank. You want to seem honest, trustworthy and dependable. Incorporate some of the elements of earth to instantly gain the interviewers trust.

Another scenario: it's Saturday night in July – but the thermometer isn't the only thing registering hot. You're up for a night on the town to meet your soul mate. Incorporate elements of fire to attract people to you. Utilizing colors, fabrics and silhouettes in your dressing rituals can be fun, enlightening and very effective. Here's to enjoying a colorful life!

Denise Butchko, AICI, is a certified fashion feng shui facilitator in Chicago who can be reached by calling 312-951-9979.

6 Keys To Color You Successful.

1. Wear colors appropriate for your industry.
2. Choose colors that either showcase you as a leader *or* a team player.
3. Choose colors that will balance and enhance your business personality.
4. Wear colors that compliment your skin tone and current hair color.
5. Wear your accent colors around your face.
6. Wear two dominant colors consistently.

Just for you . . .

List 3 appropriate colors for your industry that will work with your own coloring.

1.

2.

3.

What inspirations or insights did you get from this chapter?

> The first problem is not to learn, but to unlearn.
> Gloria Steinem

> Many accuse me of conducting
> public affairs with my heart instead of my head.
> Well, what if I do?
> Those who don't know how to weep
> with their whole heart
> don't know how to laugh either.
> Golda Meir, 1973

Unlocking The Secrets of Successful Women in Business

Key 10

What Do You Wear When . . .?

You'll find a fair amount of redundancy in here, because basic business attire is *...well... basic*. When you need to look something up quick, you'll find it all in one place.

When we conduct our two day Visual and Verbal Skill-Shops ™, the first questions always start with, "What do I wear . . .?" (For skill-shops near you, to arrange to bring a skill-shop to your company, and to subscribe to our electronic newsletter for visual and verbal tips, e-mail to: anna@personalimagesinc.com   or Linda@LindaBrakeall.com)

>
> Clothes do make the man *(or woman)*.
> Naked people have very little influence.
> Mark Twain

Linda Brakeall and Anna Wildermuth

For sales calls or job interviews?

Make sure your image enhances your message and establishes you as polished, confident, capable and credible. **Do your homework first, and then worry about what to wear.**

Wear the best accessories you can buy, including a briefcase *or* a purse, and choose a conservative simple shoe style. Color and style is based on the industry you seek employment in.

In a very casual environment such as at job sites – not office settings – wear pantsuits or slacks with coordinating sweater set, shirt with vest and if appropriate add a jacket. In office setting, wear a skirt with coordinating jacket or a suit.

If in doubt, wear an extra piece that can easily be removed to make the look more casual. It's less noticeable to remove a jacket, etc. than to add something to dress up an outfit. Example: For a company that you assume is very casual, you could wear a blazer over a soft sweater and nice slacks. If no one else is wearing a jacket, it can easily be removed. If they happened to be in suits, you'd be close if you wore a "power pin" on your lapel.

Research shows us that in more conservative areas such as the Midwest, it is safer to stick with skirted suits — rather than pantsuits — at least for the first interview. If women in powerful positions wear pantsuits where you are interviewing or selling, you can too.

Once you are hired or familiar enough with the company to understand their culture, pantsuits may be very appropriate. Linda lives in pantsuits but then *she* climbs on chairs when she is speaking and has been known to lie down on tables on a stage!

I, (Anna) always advise my clients to keep the business skirt length near the knee, depending upon your legs and height. Never more than three inches above the knee for business and then only if you are very petite and slim.

Both of us know that when you are the one seeking the job, or seeking a sale, you have to play *their* game. At least initially. There are no absolutes; these are merely our recommendations.

Tall and elegant Anna says: "Wear a dress only if it is a solid color with clean lines. Stay away from black, dark navy and red."

Shorter and curvier Linda says: "I find dresses — any dresses — lack power. Give me a suit with a jacket with shoulder pads to make me look more imposing!"

You Ask, "Do I Dress Differently When I Interview Or Do A Sales Presentation To Big, Medium And Small Clients?"

Yes! You must consider what part of the country they are from, what they respect, and what says, "competent and professional" to *them*. When we say large, medium and small, that is very subjective. One might categorize them better by corporate culture:
1. Formal
2. Informal
3. Casual

1. Large Formal Fortune 500-Type Client:

Generally speaking, you want to appear larger than life. Look for rich fabrics that hang well and do not easily wrinkle. If you own designer suits, this is the place to wear them! Your look must be well maintained with an air of easy sophistication in most fields.

Keep in mind the specific corporate culture and know your client. Remember Wal-Mart is a big client by any standard but Sam Walton was a modest man, very informal and wore his own Wal-Mart clothes. A designer suit would not have endeared you to him.

2. Medium/Informal Client:

You want to fit in. Look at what they are wearing. If they are informal, wear bridge collection (designer's off-the-rack) suits in medium toned colors. Choose moderately priced clothes that are well cut with careful attention to details such as lapels laying well, appropriate skirt, pant and sleeve length.

3. Smaller— Perhaps Casual Style— Client:

(Silicon Valley, IT and dot com companies are usually very casual, no matter their size.) You do not want to intimidate a small or casual-style client. You want to appear and sound credible but save the designer suits for the Fortune 500 companies.

You always want to blend in, but look just a wee bit better to position yourself as an expert. You don't want to overdress but you have to look like you are worth the money they will pay you. Be sensitive to their environment. Dress well in up-scale casual clothes, but leave the Rolex at home!

Are There Different Rules In Different Areas Of The Country?

Oh my yes! The savvy executive woman wears well-made clothes of good fabric that are well cut and fit well in any locale, but there are a few ways to get specific information about the local scene.

City clothes and suburban clothes may be different in the same state. Some resources:

🗝 Check out upscale magazines when they feature a city that you may do business in.

🗝 Bring several outfits. When you get there, check out the local TV news anchors. They tend to have the city's pulse.

🗝 Observe what businesswomen are wearing in restaurants if you're new to town.

🗝 Climate may influence your apparel. Always be comfortable.

🗝 The south tends to be more low-key but can be very formal in certain locations and for certain occasions.

You Ask, "What Do I Wear For An Important Meeting With A Boss, Peers, Or Co-Workers?"

In a formal business office, dress conservatively, probably in a suit. No reds or shocking trendy colors, no pastels or flower prints. You want them to take you seriously.

In warmer climates and seasons, choose lighter shades of serious colors like beiges, grays and taupes rather than navy, blacks or browns. In the colder climates and seasons, wear darker blues, olive greens and grays. Choose lighter colored blouses, sweaters, shirts or shells to soften the look and flatter your skin.

In business casual environments, choose good fabrics and well-made casual clothing. You'll probably want to wear something a notch better than the usual office wear. Perhaps adding a blazer to your shirt and pants would give you the edge.

Again, remember that in the term "business casual," the important word is business! Always iron your clothes or take them to the cleaners. When you look clean and well maintained — even in a casual setting — it shows you pay attention to details. Employers like that.

To Ask For A Raise?

Dress for the job you want because asking for a raise is a stepping-stone to a promotion. Choose conservative colors, and add a power accent, such a significant lapel pin. Check out high level respected role models in your company. Think: "Who would I like to be *like* in a few years?" Take note of their clothing and perhaps you can adapt some aspects so that when you ask for a raise, you look like you would fit in at the next level. If you really want to fast-track, you'll dress like *who you want to be* all the time!

For A Stressful Meeting Or Presentation?
(Was that phrase redundant? Aren't they *all* stressful?)

Always wear clothes that make you feel comfortable and self-assured. Wear soothing colors; blue and greens will help. Any color that appears in nature tends to calm the psyche.

To Professionally Present Myself At A Business Casual Conference Off - Site?

Add a jacket or a sweater set to slacks or skirt, accent with simple jewelry for a relaxed and polished professional statement. This is not the place for those wonderful outrageous shoulder-duster earrings you found at the boutique. And remember, say it with me now: "The important word in the phrase "business casual" is ......"

A Business Function Held At The Country Club?

This may be out of the office, this may be casual but it is still business. This is not the place for jeans or short-shorts and tank tops.

What does country club casual mean?

Casual pantsuits, long or short skirts with matching tops and jackets and lightweight tailored knits are all casual, feminine and business-like. Linda's sunny disposition needs help to be taken seriously. She often wears a business suit, but replaces the corporate silk blouse with a soft sweater. It softens the look without sacrificing the authority. Anna's serious demeanor *always* looks more business-like and she can take a softer approach, with a sweater set and slacks.

During the day, stay with skirts that hover near the knee with a jacket, or a dress or pantsuit. At night you might wear a long skirt with complementing blouse and sweater.

To A Golf Outing Or Tournament?

At country clubs, check with the pro-shop at the club for the dress rules. Most clubs do not allow any denim, tee shirts, or sweatshirts.

Casual, golf or sports wear:

If you're trying to impress colleagues or clients on the golf course, buy only the best quality, well-fitted apparel. The term is "casual" not "sloppy!" Watch for sales, and check out up-scale resale shops for shorts, sweaters with matching vests and shells, casual slacks, and resort wear at reasonable prices.

Classic golf outfit:

The stand-by basic is a solid colored shirt with cuffed sleeves and matching walking shorts, (solids, stripes or plaids, no shorter than three inches above the knee) to which you may add a tailored vee neck or a crew neck sweater. Golf shoes are spikeless leather saddle shoes with slim toes. (Nike, Foot Joy, Lady Fairway and Etonic have wonderful golf and sport shoes.) Wear low ankles socks if you are average height, (5'4") or taller, otherwise wear nearly invisible Peds. Add a coordinated visor to keep the sun and your hair out of your eyes and you're all set. Carry a vest or sweater to add a fresh look to your outfit when you go into the clubhouse and to keep your teeth from chattering in sub-zero air conditioning.

Unlocking The Secrets of Successful Women in Business

Fore Women Only
Anna And Golf

I started playing golf in 1981. It was one the best decisions I have ever made! I started playing golf to appease my husband and to get some fresh air and exercise and to enjoy nature. That husband is long-gone but the benefits of the fresh air and exercise are still there. And it has been wonderful for business!

Repeatedly I have found that playing 9 to 18 holes of golf with a potential client gives me an opportunity to get acquainted on a relaxed, unguarded basis, a chance to discover how they react to stress and to winning and losing. Last summer I was entertaining three people from an important client-company. One of our foursome was the corporate counsel and he was having absolutely the worst golfing day of his life.

On the first hole, he put three balls in the water and the third shot barely cleared the tee. He stayed calm and proceeded to hit the ball until it was over the water. Throughout the whole round of golf, he kept his good humor and didn't obsess over errors. *That* told me that he wouldn't get crazy if our project had a wrinkle or two in development.

I would love to be able to play golf with every prospect before he or she becomes a client. It would give me a chance to experience how they react to winning, losing and to frustration. If I don't like their reactions on the golf course, I won't like them any better on the job!

Another reason you might want to take up the glorious game of golf is that proportionally there are very few women playing. If you can play reasonably decently, you'll get invited to play with "the boys."

The real key is to keep up and don't complain about your golf game. An enormous amount of business is discussed on the golf course that never makes it to the boardroom. Keep current about the premier golf events, like the US Open and PGA championships and know the hot players such as Tiger Woods so you can discuss golf with some confidence and knowledge.

> Golf is a game whose aim
> is to hit a very small ball into an even smaller hole,
> with weapons singularly ill- designed for the purpose.
> Winston Churchill

To get started:

– Call your local park district, golf club or country club and ask about group or individual lessons. Make an appointment to meet the instructor. Is this someone you could work with and learn from?

– Think of golf equipment as an investment in your future as a businesswoman. After learning about quality by looking at lots of golf equipment, purchase graphite shafts in woods and possibly in irons, in the middle price range.

– Choose a medium sized lightweight golf bag because you may have to carry it. The bag will hold not only golf clubs, but also golf shoes and rain gear. *Yes, men play in the rain and you don't want to be left behind.*

– Plan to spend around $1,000 for clubs, bag and one golf outfit including shoes. For your first set, consider used golf clubs. There are great deals in the newspaper ads, used sports equipment stores and sometimes at the golf stores. You can find reasonably priced equipment at Edwin Watts - a nationwide discount chain store, or Golfsmith, a nationwide discount golf chain store.

You say, "I don't play golf. Can I play something else at these events?"

Participate in any sport or activity where you can display some degree of competence and comfort. If your group likes racket ball, tennis or running, make an effort to take lessons and practice at the park district or health club.

Research with an instructor, read a magazine or go on the Internet to learn the appropriate clothes and equipment. Find outfits that are flattering and comfortable and avoid sloppy or skimpy tops. Full figured women might have a man's shirt altered and shortened for a tidy, tailored over-shirt.

> **If our people are to fight their way up out of bondage we must arm them with the sword and the shield and the buckler of pride. *(And a golf club! AW)***
> **Mary McLeod Bethune**

For exercising, running, tennis or racket ball:

🔑 Wear shorts no shorter than five inches above the knee.

🔑 Shorts should never be tight across the stomach or too snug in the crotch.

🔑 Choose medium to darker colors to look slimmer.

🔑 Tops should not be low cut or snug across the bust. Avoid sports clothes with advertising slogans.

🔑 Shoes should be designated for the specific sports; Addias and Nike are good brands. Choose athletic shoes with some color rather than all white shoes.

🔑 Sport bras belong *under* tee shirts or polo shirts.

🔑 Keep jewelry to a minimum. (Venus Williams can do her thing, because she is a famous tennis star.)

🔑 Don't wear worn or old outfits.

🔑 Head Gear, Liz Sport and The Gap provide great sport clothes.

What to wear for swimming?

🔑 No bikinis. One-piece swimsuit with a conservative front and back.

🔑 Buy swimsuits one size larger than regular size.

🔑 Always wear a cover-up or a shirt over your suit walking to the pool.

🔑 Have swim shoes or sandals.

🔑 Keep jewelry to a minimum.

🔑 Wear a pair of shorts over your swimsuit if you feel bare and don't plan to swim. You can still join others at the beach or by the pool to socialize.

Linda Brakeall and Anna Wildermuth

You ask, "What do I wear to dinner parties?"

Find out what the hostess is wearing, and try to wear something similar. If in doubt, describe your outfit to the hostess and ask if it would be suitable.

Yikes! It's A "Black Tie" Business Event!

Usually during the week, the attire for women tends to less formal - even if it does *say* "black tie." Dressy suits, even business suits with nice jewelry, and street-length conservative dresses are more the norm with perhaps the addition of more festive shoes. The outfit can be more formal with finer fabric.

A black tie business dinner with dancing on a Friday suggests a short cocktail dress. On weekends, a long dress is appropriate. When going alone, short is better than long to maintain a business-focused appearance.

No low cut dresses or cleavage, especially if you are attending without your husband or "significant other." Stay away from hot pink, orange or shocking colors. You want them to remember *you*, not that sassy little flame colored, rhinestone infested, cut down to *there* dress! Avoid sexy, seductive outfits because… **"We're here for business!"**

> People are really quite remarkable when
> they start thinking they can do things.
> When they believe in themselves,
> they have the first secret of success.
> **Norman Vincent Peale**

It's Black Tie Optional – That's Really Confusing!

Coordinate with your date or escort, if you'll be part of a twosome. If he wears a dinner jacket/tux then dress more formally. If he wears a suit, wear a dressy suit or a silky or delicate knit dress with glamorous accessories. For drama, your ensemble should be very dark or very light. If you're going alone, choose a dressy business suit with elegant earrings, etc.

For A Television Interview?

If you become a "visible success," you may get your very own 15 minutes of fame and may well find yourself as a TV guest.

If you haven't seen the show, call ahead and ask the producer what the set looks like and what colors look best with the show's set. If possible, watch the program to see what the hosts wear. Usually plums, blues and greens look great on TV. No blacks or bright neon colors, and avoid bright white, it doesn't like cameras. If you haven't seen the set, and can't get the information in advance, take a light outfit *and* a dark outfit. (One of our friends wore her best navy blue suit to an interview and discovered the back drape of the set was navy. She looked like an eerie floating head.)

Very few American TV shows offer you professional makeup. TV lights laser-beam right through regular make-up and at least two layers of skin so you'll need a pancake-type makeup and don't forget powder. Shiny skin not only looks unattractive on TV, it looks amateurish. Let the rest of your make-up be just a bit more "definite," and wear a bit more mascara. Wear non-glare, non-dangly and non-clanky, jewelry and non-glare glasses. Cameras and microphones don't like those things.

Linda Brakeall and Anna Wildermuth

For A Radio Interview?

We know you think, "W*ho cares*, they can't see me." Chicago radio personality Catherine Johns said people often came into the studio and asked, "Why are you always dressed up? No one can see you." Catherine said, "I can see me and I know I feel more professional dressed up. That comes right through the microphone." Radio star and media coach Joel Roberts says, "To sound your best, wear your best clothes." We totally agree. Not only will you feel wonderful, you will make an impression on the host and all those around you. Dress as if you have a meeting with the chairman of the board. This is true even if you are doing the radio interview from your own home office. Dress up and smile, so your voice will project professionalism.

If I'm Running For Political Office?

You must look sharp all the time. *All the time.* Even when you are buying groceries, or on your way home from the gym. So get some decent casual clothes that you won't be embarrassed to be seen in. Because you *will* be seen at the most inconvenient times. Look at the successful women candidates in your district or state. See what works for them.

> *Your potential voters will be voting or not voting for you even when you only wanted to get milk.*
> *Look the part --- all the time!*

Leaders, whether in the family, in business,
in government, or in education,
must not allow themselves to mistake intentions
for accomplishments.
Jim Rohn

Tips for political debates and official public appearances:

Wear simple jewelry. A few nice, conservative pieces of real gold or silver. We don't want your constituents wondering if their contributions contribute to your collection of "jewels."

When it comes to suits, stick with classic and middle of the road labels called "bridge collections" such as Jones of New York, DKNY and Kasper. Bridge collections are the designer lines made for the upscale masses. Stay away from the very expensive designers. You want to look credible, dependable and cost effective. This is where a personal shopper from the best store in town can be a godsend. Tell her what you need and let her watch for it to go on sale.

Anna says: "Always wear a skirt, (rather than pants) that is easy to maintain, wrinkle free and very comfortable."

Linda says: "If your voters are highly conservative, skirts may be the safer route. But if you are spending all your time remembering to sit "like a lady," you may not nail the point in the debate. Use common sense and do what works best for you."

If Elected To A Board?

Corporations

These boards usually meet for lunch or breakfast. Wear your best corporate outfit. You want to be taken seriously. If the rest of the board dresses very casually, you can still dress with power. For more authority, always have a jacket, sweater vest or cardigan to go with slacks or a skirt. Jewelry sets the tone so choose good quality pieces with clean, uncluttered lines.

Volunteer for projects and committees. You'll learn a lot, get to know some people very well, and establish a track record as someone who gets things done. It's a wonderful way to accelerate your career.

Charitable boards

The same rules apply as for corporations: Volunteer, work hard, and get to know the people who can help you and teach you. These boards tend to meet in the evening and sometimes have a higher profile. Be consistent in your dress to send a consistent, positive message about your habits.

If they meet right after work for dinner, your office clothes should be appropriate for the board meeting with a little fine-tuning to fit the board. If they are very casual, take off your jacket. Lighter colors convey a more casual effect and pants let you be more relaxed. If they tend to be more formal than what you usually wear to work, add a jacket and perhaps some jewelry.

Anna says: "I've been on several charitable boards. I was often the youngest member, so I usually wore a suit for a little more credibility."

5 Keys To Wearing The "Right Thing:"

1. If you don't know, ask or observe what is around you.
2. Create a basic uniform for formal business dress, business casual and dress-up occasions.
3. Use accessories to dress up or dress down an outfit.
4. Dress in layers. A jacket or cardigan can be removed if the occasion is more casual than expected.
5. Choose three season fabrics for comfort and flexibility.

Unlocking The Secrets of Successful Women in Business

Just for you . . .

List 3 ways to make sure your wardrobe is ready for various business occasions.

1.

2.

3.

What do you need to STOP doing in order to look professional all the time?

What inspirations or insights did you get from this chapter?

What else do you need to know? We might be able to help.
Email us. anna@personalimagesinc.com
　　　　　Linda@LindaBrakeall.com

**There never will be complete equality until women themselves help to make laws and elect lawmakers.
Susan B. Anthony**

Linda Brakeall and Anna Wildermuth

Key 11

Traveling On Business

If you travel all the time, skip this part! You already know 95% of it. If you're traveling with others for three days or less, try to get by with only a carry on. You don't want to hold everyone up waiting for your luggage.

Find some good-looking walking shoes that can be worn with a suit (not gym shoes) to dash through airports and parking lots. If you try to walk those one to three miles in heels, or even flats without support, you'll arrive tired.

Linda says: "I often do week-long conventions in 2 - 3 suits, with 2 or 3 blouses or sweaters to go with each suit. Suit pants with a sweater set works for "after hours" gatherings and saves packing more stuff. Aim to work around one core color, so you only have to take 2 pair of good looking, comfortable shoes to cover all bases."

Wear an outfit on the plane that can be mixed and matched with other clothing you have packed. If the travel agenda is strictly casual, bring all casual clothing but if your business trip consists of meetings, sales calls, or client entertaining, the clothes you pack should have that focus.

Your carry-on bag should contain items that will allow you to operate for a day or two if your luggage is lost. (And something to answer the door in, if your luggage comes in the middle of the night.) This bag should have your toiletry essentials, makeup, and one or two items to add to the outfit you wore on the plane. Linda has had two occasions when this policy saved her from disaster. "I always travel in something I can work in…if I have to."

It's also a good idea to tuck in a bottle of water and a breakfast bar or a package of nuts to tide you over if your plane is late, you can't get food, or need a bedtime snack.

Travel broadens your horizons
and sometimes your hips.

What To Pack:

Always have a special set of travel items already packed so that you can just toss in your clothes and shoes and *go*.

- Vitamins, prescriptions, allergy meds, pain etc.
- Complete make-up kit.
- All the hair stuff (spray, rollers/curling iron etc.).
- Complete toiletry kit including: deodorant, moisturizer, toothbrush, toothpaste, dental floss, and mouthwash.

- Something to sleep in.
- Earplugs if strange noises bother you in hotels. *And they really improve the quality of life on airplanes and in airports!*
- Exercise clothes and shoes if you work out.
- Lighted cordless travel alarm clock.
- Small magnified and lighted make-up mirror.
- Extension cord with multiple plugs.
- Tiny first aid kit.
- Tiny sewing kit with pre-threaded needles.
- Collect sample-sized everything and refill the tiny bottles.

Basics For A Three-Day Business Trip Plus One Outfit To Wear On The Plane.

Choose lightweight pieces that fit you comfortably and seldom wrinkle.

- 1 suit.
- 2 - 3 pants or skirts, (one casual – perhaps shorts?) that co-ordinates with your suit.
- 1 sweater set or an extra jacket.
- 3 - 4 blouses, shells, sweaters.
- 2 - 3 pair of shoes.
- Underwear for each day plus 2 extra.
- 1 lightweight jogging suit for working out, sleeping in, or wearing as a cover-up.
- Lightweight trench coat or blazer to wear while traveling.

Unlocking The Secrets of Successful Women in Business

For A Seven To Ten Day Trip.

You will wear most items two or more times, making your outfits more interesting by mixing, matching, and accessorizing when appropriate. To the previous list, add:

🔑 1 - 2 more suits, depending upon how much business you'll be conducting.

🔑 Another coordinating jacket or a finishing piece (i.e. a vest, cardigan, scarf, or sweater) that will team up with your existing travel clothes.

🔑 Another pair of coordinating pants or a skirt.

🔑 2 - 4 more blouses, shells or lightweight sweaters. They don't take up much space and they'll freshen you up fast.

> **A journey of a thousand miles begins with one step.**
> **Take it.**
> **Anonymous**

At least three days before traveling, hang/lay out clothes you plan to take. This will give you an opportunity to pare down or add to your selection. If in doubt, leave it out! Keep in mind the climate and specific dress habits at your destination as well as the specific events you'll attend.

Bring only the fine jewelry you wear all the time. This is not the place to bring the heirloom pieces that have been in your family since the Mayflower.

Packing tip: Slip a plastic dry cleaner's bag over skirt or pants on a hanger. Next, put a blouse on same hanger, put a second plastic dry cleaner's bag over blouse. Put jacket over blouse. Put a third dry cleaner's bag over the jacket. Usually things arrive wrinkle free and ensembles are already assembled.

Linda Brakeall and Anna Wildermuth

Safety Tips:

Be sure you make four copies of credit cards, traveler's checks, driver's license, passport, photo ID, etc. Keep one at the office with an assistant who can fax it to you if necessary, one at home for your record, one on your person, and one in your luggage. A friend lost all her luggage and had no way to prove who she was in Mexico. Make sure *you* have a back up plan.

Buy a cloth travel wallet that holds a credit card and some cash to be worn inside your clothes...just in case!

Travel Tips
By Guest Columnist The Savvy Traveller

– Wear dark clothes with light or bright accents. Build a travel wardrobe. Layer clothes. Mix and match.

– Put a copy of your itinerary and your name, home or business address and telephone numbers in each piece of baggage. In case of lost luggage, emergencies, etc. This will save time and aggravation.

– Carry at least one major credit card and an ATM card.

– Carry a telephone calling card so you will have an alternative if your cell phone won't work.

– Be aware of everything going on around you.

– Drink lots of water while flying.

– Keep a bag of essentials permanently packed to "grab and go."

– Plan. Know where you're going, how you're getting there, the weather, functions and activities attending etc.

The Savvy Traveller, a retail store filled with books, maps, and all manner of things that make travel and packing easier and more fun. 310 South Michigan, Chicago, IL. www.thesavvytraveller.com.

Unlocking The Secrets of Successful Women in Business

Just for you . . .

What are 3 ways to make it easier on you when you travel?

1.

2.

3.

What do you need to STOP doing to simplify traveling?

What inspirations or insights did you get from this chapter?

What else do you need to know? We might be able to help.
Email us. anna@personalimagesinc.com
        Linda@LindaBrakeall.com

Don't accept rides from strange men
--and remember that all men are strange as hell.
Robin Morgan

Think wrongly, if you please,
but in all cases think for yourself.
Doris Lessing

Linda Brakeall and Anna Wildermuth
Key 12

Buying The Right Professional Clothes

Learn About Quality Clothing At The Best Department Store In Town.

Think Nordstrom, Bloomingdale's, Saks' etc. Try on different brands and designers until you find what suits your figure, your wallet and your business. After you've learned the rules at the best store in town, you may be able to find the right stuff at more reasonable prices by shopping sales, outlets or re-sale stores.

To consistently look like a well put-together professional, buy fewer pieces of better clothing rather than more clothes of lesser quality. Find a personal shopper you like and trust at one of those stores and honestly tell her your situation: What you need, how much you can spend etc. Personal shoppers will often call you when "your" suit goes on sale and maybe you will be able to afford something luxurious. She'll also be able to tell you where you can economize and how to "pull together" an outfit, so you'll look and feel wonderful rather than merely acceptable.

Make sure it fits.

A suit that really fits you well always looks like it costs twice as much! To get a really good fit, your professional wardrobe may have to be tailored. The better stores have tailors, and perhaps your dry cleaner does that as well. Ask your friends for recommendations.

Does The Suit *Suit* You?
Courtesy Of E-How.com

– Select a suit color and pattern. Black, navy and gray are all classic tones. If you opt for a patterned suit, check that the patterns line up at the seams of the shoulders and lapels.

– Choose a suit fabric. High-quality worsted wool is seasonally versatile; avoid blends with too much polyester.

– Crumple the fabric to see if it bounces back instead of remaining wrinkled.

– Pick a jacket style. The single-breasted suit is classic, but there are also double-breasted suits, and those that button to the collar.

– Determine your preferred jacket length. Pockets can be besom (slit), flap or patch; besom pockets are formal, while patch pockets provide a casual look.

– Decide between a skirt and pants, or buy both. The traditional skirt suit is appropriate in highly formal business settings, but the relaxed pantsuit is sometimes acceptable. It might be practical to buy a three-piece set: jacket, skirt and pants.

– Select your pants style. Pleats make pants dressy and provide room to move around, while flat-front pants are slimming. Cuffed legs are formal and add weight to the suit; uncuffed pants elongate the leg.

– Test for jacket fit. Make sure the collar lies flat against the back of your neck. Shoulders should be lightly padded and neither too boxy nor sloped. Sleeves should reveal 1/4 to 1/2 inch of dress cuff or fall five inches above the tip of your thumb.

– Make sure the skirt or pants fit. You should be able to slide two fingers under the waistline and pull about 1 inch of excess fabric at the hip. Skirts should fall straight. Back, not side zippers help a skirt to fall more smoothly. Pay attention to the crotch area for pants, making sure it lies perfectly flat against your body.

– Consider your body shape and the silhouette you would like to achieve with the suit.

– Women with straight, angular bodies might prefer suits with straight lines. Search for longer jackets that have sharp lapels and are not too cinched at the waist.

– Women with curvy bodies should wear suits with rounded lines: a fitted waist, shorter jacket, curved lapel and skirt with rounded bottom.

– Don't forget to check for suit quality. Well-made suits have full linings, neatly finished hems and hand-sewn buttonholes (Identifiable by their irregular stitching).

Reprinted with permission from www.e-how.com

Fabrics:

For business-wear look first at lightweight gabardines, heavy suede silks, combination polyester with cotton, and wool and rayon blends. Cheaper fabrics look almost-as-good the first few times they are worn but quickly look shabby after repeated washings or cleanings. A $60 blouse may last 6 times longer than a $20 blouse, but only cost 3 times as much.

All-natural fabrics feel better but wrinkle more. All-synthetic blends wrinkle less but are far less comfortable than natural fabrics because synthetics like polyester and acrylics do not breathe. (Remember how "sticky" rayon often feels?) Designers are using synthetic-natural blends more often to get the best of both.

The choice of fabric often indicates formal or casual wear. For example, a silk tee shirt may go under a designer suit; a cotton tee shirt will go with jeans. A wool suit goes to the office and the same suit made in silk can go to black tie dinners.

Check Fabric And Stitching Before You Buy
Courtesy Of E-How.com

– Inspect fabrics to make sure that patterns line up at the seams, at the shoulder, collar and pocket.

– Hold fabric up to light and make sure weave is tight, even and uniform, with no loose or undone threads. If fabric has beads or sequins, make sure that they're securely attached.

– Check the grain of the fabric. Its vertical grain should run straight up and down the garment, and the horizontal grain should run at a 90-degree angle to this line.

– Crumple the fabric to see if it bounces back, either immediately or in several minutes, indicating resistance to wrinkling.

– Rub two layers of fabric together to check for pilling (the formation of small fiber balls).

– Compare fabric lengths: fold pants, shirts, skirts and other garments in half to ensure that fabric is symmetrical in length between the right and left sides.

– Verify that all stitches are secure and straight. You should see about 8 to 12 stitches per inch.

– Examine hems, which should be nearly invisible. Hemmed bottoms should hang straight and not curl.

– Check that right and left collars are equal in length and have symmetrical, or mirror-imaged, patterns.

– Pockets should lie perfectly flat against the cloth, with no gaps.

– Hold up clothing to ensure that the lining follows the cut of the garment, falls smoothly and does not extend below the hemline. In general, women's pants are fully lined, while men's pants are lined only in front to just below the knees.

– Armholes should sit no more than 1 1/2 inches below the armpit.

– Verify that buttons and buttonholes are sewn tightly, with no unraveled thread. In general, the more buttons a shirt has, the higher quality it is. Also check whether the shirt has spare buttons.

– Try on the shirt; button it fully, making sure buttons are placed well and that the shirt doesn't gape open across the chest.

– Pull zippers up and down a few times to make sure they run smoothly and don't snag.

– Remember to examine clothing from all sides, front and back, for possible defects.

Reprinted with permission from www.e-how.com.

You Ask, "What Are The Tailored Business Basics?"

A three-season wardrobe is the key to a consistent image.

This means you can wear the wardrobe nine months of the year and some pieces year round. Lighter colors for spring/summer and darker colors for fall/winter.

Your first major purchase needs to be a formal business suit with a "power accent." A dark suit with a high contrast blouse and a significant lapel pin sends a powerful and senior level corporate message that says, "Take me seriously!" A tailored suit without a blouse needs a scarf, pin or necklace.

Next, find a casual business suit with a jacket that can also be worn with slacks, skirt, shorts or jeans. Add a scarf or large "serious" piece of jewelry. Coordinating pieces in softer colors send a "friendlier" message than matching pieces.

You'll also need a raincoat with removable lining or a topcoat that will fit over a suit jacket. Either will take you through most weather.

Basic tops, blouses and sweaters.

Select 2 – 4 tops for each suit or outfit to vary your look, in solids or prints. Stay away from prints for main pieces, but they are great as accents. Depending upon your body shape and profession, start with some 100% cotton oxford or knit shirts, some silk or silky shirts or blouses, and a few shells in cotton or silk.

If you have trouble finding blouses that match your suits well, *and you never take off your jacket,* look for scarves to drape and pin over a camisole to give you that *LA Law drape-neck blouse* look. Next, check out a matching sweater set for a finished but less-formal look.

Note: Anna loves sweater sets and oxford shirts because she has a tall, thin elegant body. Linda never wears either because she has an hourglass figure and feels like Dolly Parton in those items. In fact, Linda scrupulously avoids business blouses with buttons in front because sometimes they gape - no matter the size.

> "They can't take you seriously
> if they're looking at your underwear!"
> Linda Brakeall

Coordinating pieces:

Stick with a few basic colors as your wardrobe foundation; and choose pieces that you *know* you will use. Your next essential is a good blazer or jacket that will go with other pieces you already own, and maybe dress up casual slacks, too. Buy a few well-made dress pants and skirts that will work with the jackets you already have. By the way, jeans need to be replaced ASAP with Dockers, khaki's or chinos for professional casual wear.

Next, gather some more casual tops like soft, lightweight sweaters in solid colors, and washable dressy tee shirts in a stretch fabric or silk. The office is not the place for those cotton-wear-with-jeans tee-shirts.

Illustrations of basic tops from left:
Turtleneck sweater, mock turtle, and polo shirt.

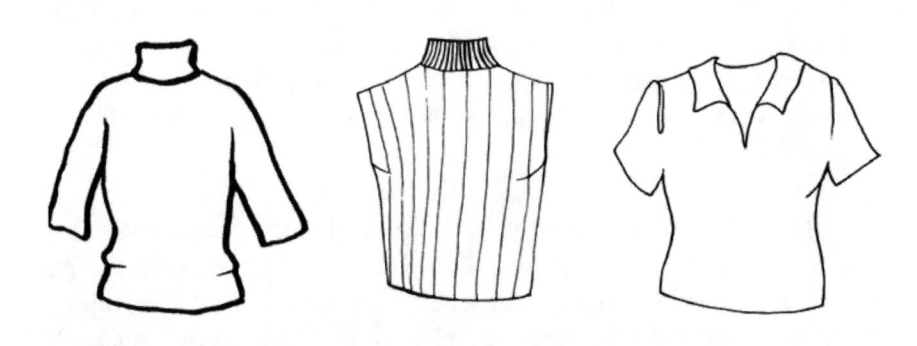

Illustrations of jackets from left:
Collarless Chanel-look, open front jacket, wrap jacket for tall and hourglass figures.

Unlocking The Secrets of Successful Women in Business

Illustrations from left:
Short sporty jacket, 4-button boxy jacket,
and traditional 2-button, slightly fitted jacket.

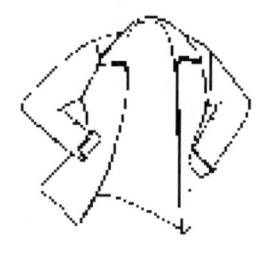

Illustrations of basic bottoms from left:
Flat-front slacks for the flat-tummied, slim skirt, and flounce-skirt.

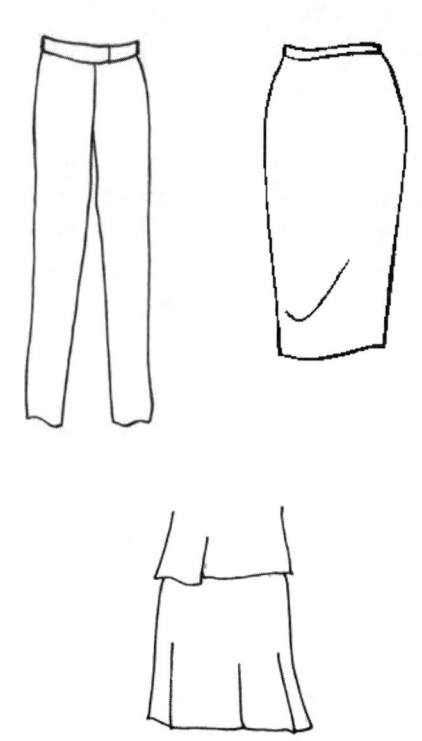

Linda Brakeall and Anna Wildermuth

You ask, "How Much Should I Pay For My Clothes?"

"Different strokes for different folks" is the first thing that comes to mind. You can look appropriate and professional on any budget.

Recently I (Anna) took an office equipment sales associate shopping. She had less than $300 available for new professional clothes. We went to Nordstrom's Rack and purchased one pant-suit, and one skirted-suit, four cotton shells, two pair of casual pants from a sale rack for $10.00 each, two pair of dress slacks, one belt and one casual jacket. The bill came to $285.00. All were good quality blends of wool and poly. We stayed within her budget and she looked wonderful. Just those few items took her professionalism up 100%! Her CEO could not get over the transformation when we added a new haircut, glasses and makeup.

I've had other senior level and high profile clients who spend an average of $1500 on a suit. Their social circles recognize the designer and are aware of the quality, but less-wealthy clients and customers never notice the price tag because they are always so appropriately understated and elegant.

> Class is an aura of confidence
> that is being sure without being cocky.
> Class has nothing to do with money.
> Class never runs scared.
> It is self-discipline and self-knowledge.
> It's the sure footedness
> that comes with having proved you can meet life.
> **Ann Landers**

Savvy Shopping For A Professional Wardrobe.

Power shopping basics

Before you actually go shopping to *buy*, you must figure out what you already have, and make a list of what you'll need to complete your professional wardrobe. Shop early in the day while you are fresh with a flexible plan.

🔑 Buy shoes last, after your feet are tired and swollen. If shoes feel good after a day of shopping, they'll feel good anytime!

🔑 Shop alone or with an objective friend who will stay focused on what you need to buy.

🔑 Resist impulse buying.

🔑 If you find a wonderful item, make sure that you have at least three pieces that you can wear with it, or buy three new pieces to make it into an "outfit."

🔑 Buy basics such as panties, bras, hose, socks etc. in bulk, and on sale, by catalog, phone or the Internet if you know the brand and it fits.

🔑 Establish relationships with various salespersons in different stores if you want to shop smart and shop fast.

Dress for the hunt

🔑 Wear comfortable shoes; you'll be on your feet a long time.

🔑 Wear an outfit that is easy to get in and out of, so you can try things on quickly.

🔑 Wear neutral hose that will go with everything.

🔑 Bring appropriate shoes and undergarments such as evening shoes and a strapless bra when you shop for an evening dress, or shoes to go with a suit, etc.

Should you buy it?

When you try on clothes, use the blink test: Get dressed. Close your eyes, then open them. If your first impression is: "Wow! I look great!" Buy it! If in doubt, ***don't!*** It won't improve! Secondly, it must feel good on your body. If it binds, rides up or feels "weird" in the dressing room, it won't feel any better after you get it home.

Be sure you understand what works for your profession. If you like hot pink suits but you are a corporate lawyer for a conservative practice, save the hot pink suit for your private social life, and buy the navy blue.

Ten Best Buys For Your Professional Wardrobe.

1. A pair of basic black, (or brown, gray or navy, if your wardrobe is built around one of those colors) shoes that look as good as they feel to wear with slacks or skirts.
2. A big plain square leather or fabric black tote with two straps long enough to carry on the shoulder, to hold everything from business files to shoes.
3. A sweater set unless you're "busty."
4. A well cut black straight knee-length skirt.
5. A terrific coat to last at least three years.
6. A comfortable, good-looking pair of casual pants.
7. A good watch.
8. A good pen.
9. Great underwear and enough of it.
10. Quality panty hose purchased by the dozen from a catalog or Internet outlet.

Unlocking The Secrets of Successful Women in Business

Ten Biggest Money-Wasters.

1. Cheap hose/stockings.
2. A cheap silk blouse that needs to be dry-cleaned.
3. Shoes that don't really fit and/or look a little weird but were a great buy.
4. One amazingly wonderful piece that does not go with anything else you own.
5. Pants, skirt, shirt or *anything* that is just a little too tight.
6. A blouse, dress or skirt that looks great if you don't bend over too far, reach too high or have to work for a living.
7. Cashmere, leather, silk or suede at a price you can't believe that looks and feels awful.
8. Something to wear to someone else's wedding — and nowhere else.
9. Something to wear for someone else's *life*. "Karen has one of these and she wears it all the time."
10. Anything you don't really need but it has a designer label and is marked **50% off.**

Become a possibilitarian.
No matter how dark things seem to be or actually are,
raise your sights and see possibilities --
always see them, for they're always there.
Norman Vincent Peale

Linda Brakeall and Anna Wildermuth
Buy The Right Professional Shoes

Find a few brands of shoes that feel wonderful and fit well and stick with them.

If they really fit well, they'll last longer and justify spending more money on them. Buying fewer shoes will simplify your life, your closet, and save you lots of money. Spend more money on shoes that are worn frequently and far less on occasional shoes that only work with occasional outfits.

For professional shoes, wear conservative, comfortable, simple styles. Buy versatile shoes that can be worn with skirts and slacks. Buy leather shoes first, then suede and cloth. Check out micro fiber shoes because they look great, hold up well, and cost less than leather.

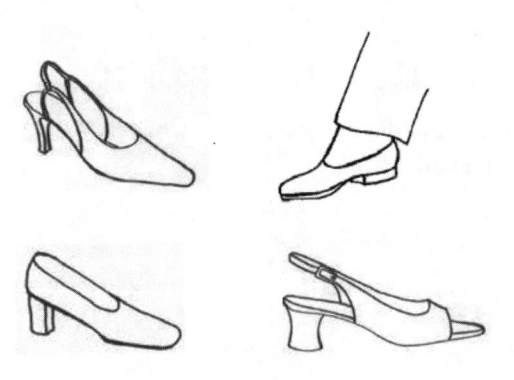

Save the 3-inch platforms and multi-color strappy sandals for vacation!

Shoes will date you or sabotage your professional image when:

🗝 Toes are too pointed or too square.

🗝 Heels are too thin or too high.

🗝 Shoes draw specific attention to your feet; so get rid of shocking-colored shoes. Let people pay attention to *you*, not your shoes.

🗝 Shiny patent leathers are good only in the evening unless you want to project that "I just got to the city and this is the first time I've worn shoes" image.

Make shoes last longer and look better.

When you buy a new pair of shoes, polish them right away and keep them polished. Shoe creams condition leather as they shine your shoes. Be careful with mink oil which can change the shine or color. No time to shine? Try the shoemaker.

Protect your suede shoes with suede spray. Brush before and after wearing and use shoetrees to help shoes keep their shape.

Check your heels at the end of every season. Have them re-heeled or re-soled when needed. When shoes no longer look good enough to be seen when you want to impress someone, give them or throw them away. Icky shoes ruin the whole look.

Buy Good Panty Hose/Stockings.

Cheap hose will look....*cheap!* No runs or snags. Not even little ones. Throw them out or wear them under pants. Hose that are too light or too dark will date your look. Please ignore weirdly colored hose in favor of natural legs in most colors of brown, off black with black outfits, and navy with navy outfits.

I saw a lady in chartreuse hose the other day. Made me wonder if she had a rare disease. Hose that are too tight or keep falling down not only ruin the look, they also interfere with your sunny disposition.

Buy The Right Handbags And Briefcases For Success.

Buy the best you can afford. Everyday handbags will last three seasons at the most. Classic special occasion evening bags can last forever. Keep them wrapped in a drawer until you need them.

Illustrations: from the left, classic tote handbag, hobo-bag, stylish feminine brief case with flap, traditional brief case.

A good briefcase can give you a lifetime of service. Keep the briefcase polished with leather lotion or take it to a good leather store to be refreshed at little or no cost. The color depends on your basic wardrobe, but darker colors, rather than lighter, are preferred if you want to be taken seriously. If you can't afford a high-quality leather briefcase, there are lots of really good-looking fabric totes that work well. I (Anna) found some recently at Target for less than $20 that I use all the time.

"Happiness is not a state to arrive at, but a manner of traveling."
Margaret Lee Runbeck

Unlocking The Secrets of Successful Women in Business
Buying Professional Jewelry.

Start collecting classic pieces you love. They will create a professional, social and economic history. Simple jewelry is never out of style. No long, dangly earrings for business! They are distracting and send a "sexy" message, which is inappropriate in most fields. Today's business jewelry tends to be simple but substantial. Pins and brooches are up to the length of your finger in size. A signature pin or necklace, worn consistently, helps you become more recognizable. By the way, wear a necklace or a pin — not both.

Good silver is better than imitation gold. Small gold pieces are often affordable if you watch for sales. It's better to have two pairs of real gold or real silver earrings than 15 pairs of costume. If you wear costume jewelry, be ready to ruthlessly discard it at the first sign of wear!

Buy a good watch that you can easily read. *Funny story:* Rita Davenport, well-known professional speaker, TV personality, with a killer southern accent says this about her watches: "You may have noticed that I'm wearing two watches. You see this one? Well, *this one* is a $10 Timex. I wear it 'cause I can *see* it." (She giggles). "And you may have noticed *this* one. It's a $10,000 Rolex. (She pauses.) I wear it 'cause *you* can see it!"

As Rita says, they *will* see it so make it a nice one! And a good pen also counts as "jewelry." Even the frames on your eyeglasses count as jewelry or an accessory.

> I went to a bookstore and asked the saleswoman,
> "Where's the self-help section?"
> She said if she told me, it would defeat the purpose.
> George Carlin

Linda Brakeall and Anna Wildermuth

Choosing The Right Eyewear Frames For Your Face
Courtesy Of Jill Dellert

Today, glasses are as much a fashion accessory as they are a necessity. Eyewear plays a big role in your life. It affects your performance and your appearance. There are many eyewear choices; each designed to fit an individual's prescription, face shape, lifestyle and personal coloring. Step into an optician's shop and you're faced with hundreds of eyeglass frames, in all shapes, sizes, colors and contours.

How do you find the best frames for your face?
"You need an unbiased opinion -- so don't trust your loved ones," cautions Jill Dellert, President of Sight Onsite Eyewear, Inc. The right optician considers your coloring, face shape and structure, (Including the placement of eyes, brows, nose and the width of your cheekbones) and hairstyle, and then adds your likes and dislikes to come up with the perfect style for you.

Your face shape
In order to determine the shape of your face, pull all of your hair back and stand about a foot away from a mirror. Take a bar of soap and outline your face on the mirror. There are seven basic facial shapes. Guidelines from the vision council of America:

The oval face is very versatile with frames because of its balanced proportions. **Frame options:** wide as or wider than the broadest part of the face -- almonds or oval-shaped frames.

The base-down triangle face has a narrow forehead and widens at the cheek and chin areas. **Frame options:** frames that draw attention upwards -- bold frames, cat-eye shapes.

The base-up triangle face (heart shaped) is widest at the forehead and narrowest at the chin. **Frame options:** frames that draw attention downwards -- rimless styles, very thin metals or plastics.

The square face is has a strong jaw line and broad forehead. Width and length are in the same proportions. **Frame options:** rounder, narrower styles that soften facial angle - narrow ovals.

The round face has curved lines, and the width and length are in the same proportions. **Frame options:** frames that are wider than they are deep -- angular, narrow frames.

The oblong face is longer than it is wide, and is characterized by a long, straight cheek line and sometimes, a longer nose. **Frame options:** frames with top-to- bottom depth or decorative temples (frame arm) to add with.

The diamond face is narrowest at the brow line and jaw line. Cheekbones are frequently high and dramatic. **Frame options:** frame with detailing or distinctive brow lines, cat-eyes or ovals.

Using eyewear to improve facial balance

Here are several techniques for using eyewear to improve facial balance:

Face: To shorten a face: try mid or low temples; deeper, narrow frames; or a low bridge. To lengthen it, try high temples; a high bridge; shallow, wide frames; or frames with little or no color on the lower rim.

Nose: to shorten a long nose, choose frames with a low or colored bridge. To lengthen a short nose, try a keyhole bridge or a high or clear bridge. To narrow and lengthen a wide nose, try a clear or metal bridge that sits close to the nose; nose pads will also help.

Eyes: To widen close-set eyes, select frames with an unobtrusive bridge. A clear bridge with darker colors placed at the outer edges of the frame is best; narrow-width frames will help to center the eyes. To narrow wide-set eyes, use a dark-colored bridge; make sure the eyes are centered in the lenses, to minimize their width.

The right frame for a large or small face

A small face is enhanced by thin metals and subtle colors; lightweight frames or a rimless style are best; don't overwhelm delicate features with heavy or exaggerated frames. Slightly oversized frames can balance a large face. Frames must be in scale with the size of the face.

Color

Skin tone is the prime element is determining coloring. All complexions fall into one of two color bases: blue (cool) or yellow (warm). A cool complexion has blue or pink undertones, and a warm one has a yellow or golden undertones. Olive skin is classified as cool, because it is a combination of both blue and yellow. In the U.S., cool, blue-based complexions are more common and make up approximately 60 percent of our population.

An individual's overall coloring is affected by one more element, high or low intensity coloring. High-intensity coloring conveys a total facial vividness that has nothing to do with make-up or the lack of it. High-intensity people are able to wear strong, primary colors successfully. Low-intensity individuals are more muted and do better with softer colors.

Linda Brakeall and Anna Wildermuth

If you wear the wrong color eyewear:
Circles under the eyes are more noticeable, producing a tired look. For men, heavy "five o'clock shadow" (at 10:00 a.m.) Shows more clearly. Skin appears yellow around the eyes and mouth. Everyone looks best in his or her own color base and eyewear color should complement personal coloring.

Eyewear is the most important accessory next to make-up.
If you have poor vision follow these do's and don'ts when applying your make-up.

The lenses for a far-sighted person will magnify the eyes.
-Don't overly exaggerated eye make-up.
-Do use subtle colors and applications.
-Don't apply heavy or clumpy mascara.
-Do groom eyebrows carefully.

The lenses for a near-sighted person will make the eyes and the area surrounding them appear smaller.
-Don't line eyes completely because it makes them appear smaller.
-Do line eyes to add width.
-Don't thin out eyebrows or make them look narrow.
-Do define eyebrows and use mascara lavishly.
-Do apply eye make-up more intensely.

Tips for speakers, on-camera appearances or photographs:
Lenses
The anti reflective coating is a lens treatment of multi-layer coating which eliminates reflection and increases light transmission. This allows people to see your eyes better and allows you to see better through your lenses, especially at night. The edges of the lenses should not be polished as this also eliminates reflection.

Frames
Select frames that have a minimalist look. Choose colors that blend with your skin tones and have a matte finish. Rimless styles are also a good choice.

Many people consider the eyes to be the most important feature of a person's style; they are the "windows to the soul." so if you wear eyeglasses, it's paramount that they complement your natural coloring, basic personal style and the basic shape of your face.

Reprinted with permission by Jill Dellert, founder and President of Sight Onsite Eyewear, Inc., Chicago, IL. 888-628-5438.

Unlocking The Secrets of Successful Women in Business

Just for you . . .

What are 3 shopping strategies you'll use next time you have to make a purchase for your professional wardrobe?

1.

2.

3.

What do you need to STOP doing in order to buy wisely?

What inspirations or insights did you get from this chapter?

What else do you need to know? We might be able to help.
Email us. anna@personalimagesinc.com
         Linda@LindaBrakeall.com

> Don't wait until everything is just right;
> it will never be perfect. Get started now.
> With each step you take,
> you will grow stronger and stronger,
> more and more skilled,
> more and more self-confident.
> Mark Victor Hansen

Linda Brakeall and Anna Wildermuth
Key 13

Professional Wardrobe Maintenance

No Matter The Cost, Clothes Seldom Stay Fresh-Looking And Current For More Than Two To Five Seasons.

The exceptions are blouses, scarves and formal wear that still fit. Eveningwear may go out of style, but sometimes it comes back. (Linda has several antique gowns that she adores.) So if you love an evening ensemble and it still fits you well, hang on to it. All the rest of your clothes, with very few exceptions, need to be given away or thrown out in two to five years.

The clothes you wear every week will seldom last more than two seasons. If you find an extraordinary suit that you adore and plan to wear over and over, you might want to buy two! Or you can extend the life by buying other pieces that you can mix and match. Outfits worn less frequently will obviously last longer.

After five years, most items tend to look faded, frayed, tired or the "look" just isn't right because shoulders, collars, lapels, skirt length, jacket length and lines change. Sometimes the changes are subtle and the outfit that was absolutely flawless five years ago now looks "funny." If you are reluctant to let go of a good suit you might use this trick from a clever friend, Sheila Glazov, author of <u>Princess Shayna's Invisible Visible Gift.</u> She has a wonderful tailor who updates all those things — collars, shoulders etc. — for her when she wants to keep clothes past their normal life span. She also replaces buttons on expensive suits to make them look new.

Linda says: *"That works, but it's too much trouble for me!"*

Anna says: *"It's worth the effort and will save you money in the long run."*

Professional Wardrobe Maintenance Check List:

Confucius said, "God is in the details." *So is your career.* Someone may think that sloppy shoes means sloppy work. So do an annual check up. . Once a year, maybe for your birthday, take inventory. Book at least a day for the review and two days for shopping and organizing. Put the plan on paper by hand or via computer

- Organize your closet and get rid of all clothing that does not fit or you have not worn in a season.

- Make sure all items in the closet are clean and ready to wear.

- Replace anything that is no longer pristine. If clothes are not in perfect condition, either have them repaired or ruthlessly discard! The acid-test question about perfect condition: "Would I be embarrassed if my best client saw me in this?"

- Make sure everything fits well with ample room. We don't want you looking like a sausage, do we?
- Are sleeve lengths too short or too long?
- Are your jackets still current or have shoulders, lapels or length changed?
- Are your skirts and pants the right length?

Closet Cleaning Rules

I (Anna) had a client who had kept clothes from high school. At forty-four, she was proud she could still get in them. She had a jam-packed 20 x 20 closet and never had anything to wear. Sound familiar?

Ruthlessly discard the following!

- Anything you have not worn in the last year.
- Anything that doesn't fit, or isn't comfortable. I said be ruthless!
- Anything you "know will come back in style." *Fuhgeddaboudit*! If it does come back, it will come back in another version. The only exceptions are jewelry, classic blouses, sweaters and scarves.
- Anything that you feel tacky in or that you know is not your color. It will never feel any better. If you feel tacky, you won't be working up to your potential.
- Anything that is faded, worn, torn, stained, pilled, snagged, stretched or shapeless. **If in doubt, toss it out!**
- Make sure all shoes and coats are still current and in perfect condition. Check your accessories, too, such as belts, scarves, and watches. Check jewelry to be sure clasps and stones are tight.

Unlocking The Secrets of Successful Women in Business

Tip for die-hard pack rats: Gather up all the clothes you haven't worn in three seasons but you hate to part with because they still fit and are in excellent condition. Put a date on the bag. Any item that you don't wear within a year from today, give away. Charities are always looking for clothes. Set those good clothes free to help another woman.

Clothing care.

🗝 Always hang up clothes on padded hangers immediately after wearing.

🗝 Air out your clothes to extend their wear and keep them smelling fresh, not of food, mothballs or old perfume.

🗝 Remove all pins and jewelry from lapels etc.

🗝 Store less-frequently worn garments in garment bags that are *not* plastic. Plastic bags have been known to change the colors on some fabrics in just a few months. The colors do not change evenly and it is not a good look.

🗝 If possible dry-clean no more than two to three times per season because it wears out your clothing. Learn to spot clean and have items professionally pressed. Freshen sweaters and knits in the dryer with a sheet of fabric softener to save wear and tear at the dry cleaners.

> One cannot collect
> all the beautiful shells on the beach.
> Anne Morrow Lindbergh

Linda Brakeall and Anna Wildermuth

5 Keys To Maintaining A Professional Wardrobe:

1. All clothing must be clean and fragrance free.
2. All clothing must fit well.
3. Keep most clothes no more than three seasons.
4. Review wardrobe each spring and fall.
5. Add one new outfit each year to update.

> Poor is the person who depends
> upon the permission of another.
> Madonna

> Women never have a half-hour in all their lives
> (excepting before or after anybody is up in the house)
> that they can call their own, without fear of offending
> or of hurting someone.
> Why do people sit up so late, or,
> more rarely, get up so early?
> Not because the day is not long enough,
> but because they have "no time in the day
> to themselves."
> Florence Nightingale in 1852

Unlocking The Secrets of Successful Women in Business

Just for you . . .

List 3 actions steps to ensure that your professional wardrobe is always in top condition:

1.

2.

3.

What do you need to STOP doing in order to keep your professional wardrobe in top condition?

What inspirations or insights did you get from this chapter?

What else do you need to know? We might be able to help Email us.   anna@personalimages.inc.com
              Linda@LindaBrakeall.com

You have to leave room in life to dream.
Buffy Sainte-Marie

S.I.L.L.Y.
Self Imposed Limitations Lie to You
Anonymous

Linda Brakeall and Anna Wildermuth

Key 14

The Shapes Of Goddesses.

Six Basic Figure Shapes

Isn't it nice to think of your self as a goddess?
When we listed our friends in terms of goddess body types, we were amazed at how many matched the following descriptions – perhaps you do too.

Even within these basic shapes, there is still a lot of diversity. Your body can be generous or thin, tall or short; your bra cup can be overflowing or padded. Each body has its challenges and assets.

Hourglass or Aphrodite, the goddess of love and beauty. She represents woman's enjoyment of life.

Rectangle or Persephone, the maiden queen of the under world who wants to be wanted.

Unlocking The Secrets of Successful Women in Business

Triangle or Demeter, the goddess of grain. She is maternal (wide hips) and has a drive to provide physical and spiritual sustenance.

Inverted triangle or Artemis is the goddess of the hunt (wide shoulders), independent feminine spirit.

Apple or Hestia who is the goddess of the hearth. She is patient and offers comfort and wholeness.

Average. You don't have a goddess, but you can buy and wear clothes easier than the rest of us. That seems to me to be sufficient recompense!

> **After thirty the body has a mind of its own.**
> **Bette Midler**

Determining Your Shape.

It's really simple. Go to a good department store that sells coordinated separates. Find an outfit that you like. Take the same outfit in three sizes into the dressing room; your usual size plus one smaller and one larger than you usually wear. More about sizes, including size charts in the next chapter.

If your usual size is too tight or too big anywhere, try one of the other sizes and see if you can get a comfortable fit with a larger or smaller top. Then try the same for the bottom. If it's too long, try Petites. Too short? Try Talls. Too tight? Try Woman's or Plus Sizes. This is the time to explore and find the right size for you. You might be a Petite on top, and a Misses on the bottom, or some other previously unconsidered combination.

If you wear the same size top and bottom, but ***the waist of the garment is obviously too big,*** you are an hourglass or Aphrodite

If you wear the same size top and bottom, but **the waist of the garment is too tight**, you are probably a rectangle or Persephone.

If you need a larger bottom, you are a triangle or Demeter.

If you need a larger top, you are an inverted triangle or Artemis.

If you have a very obvious tummy, you are an apple or Hestia.

If you are pregnant, follow the apple tips.

If one size fits you well, top, bottom and waist, then bless your heart, you're average, and we're jealous!

Your Basic Shape Is Your Basic Shape.

You may be 89 pounds or several multiples of that. The rules will still apply and you will modify them according to your height and weight.

You can be attractive, professional and appealing in any size, height or weight if you take the time to learn the rules and make just a few modifications.

> Everything's in the mind.
> That's where it all starts.
> Knowing what you want
> is the first step toward getting it.
> Mae West

Unlocking The Secrets of Successful Women in Business

Aphrodite - Hour Glass

Well-defined waist, 1/3 smaller than bust and hip measurement. That would be 12 – 8 – 12 in a doll. Bust and hips are similar measurements.

Aphrodite will fit best in soft curved-line garments. Hourglass figures are seldom found in single-digit sizes. Did you know that Marilyn Monroe was a size 14? And Mae West was larger than that. Those were definitely hourglass figures and they flaunted them!

For years, Linda wore boxy jackets trying to obscure the oh-so-obvious bosom and bottom that goes with the hourglass shape. AA, *After Anna*, she wears fitted jackets most of the time and everyone asks: "Have you lost a lot of weight?" Choose suit jackets, and other clothes that are shaped to indicate the waist-line and often shoulder pads add balance.

Famous Aphrodites:

Dolly Parton

Elizabeth Taylor

Linda Brakeall

Ivana Trump

Marilyn Monroe

Mae West

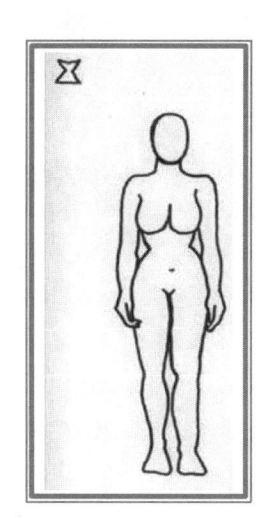

Linda Brakeall and Anna Wildermuth

The Hour Glass Body Will Be Flattered By:

🔑 Soft, curved line garments.

🔑 Sculpted, fitted jackets and dresses with deep darts for bust and waist.

🔑 Jacket length typically between wrist and no longer than fingertip, never ending at fullest part of hip.

🔑 Raglan sleeves.

🔑 Narrower sleeves on jackets and narrower bottoms on pants-leg.

🔑 Soft draping, bias-cut fabrics such as knits, in cotton, wool, rayon and blends will fit naturally against your body. Soft gabardines in wool/viscose blends mold your body.

I believe the greatest gift I can conceive
of having from anyone is to be seen, heard,
understood and touched by them.
The greatest gift I can give is to see, hear,
understand and touch another person.
When this is done, I feel contact has been made.
Virginia Satir

Unlocking The Secrets of Successful Women in Business

Persephone - Rectangle Shape

Same width shoulders and hips, less-defined waist.

In larger sizes, it is easy to confuse rectangles with apples. See *apple* for further definition. Persephones can be elegant and classic. Coco Chanel was probably a rectangle, because her clothes fit Persephone so well. The challenge for Persephone is to minimize attention to the waist area.

Famous Persephones:

Julia Roberts

Gwyneth Paltrow

Anna Wildermuth

Diane Sawyer

Audrey Hepburn

Jackie Kennedy Onassis

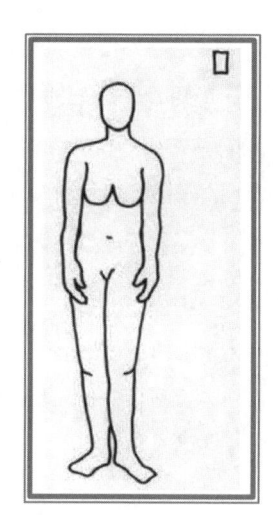

Persephone will be flattered by:

🗝 Garments, suit jackets and dresses where the lines and shapes are straighter up and down.

🗝 "Chanel" boxy jacket, with a straight skirt.

🗝 Straight long jackets with short skirts.

🗝 The "chemise" or "sack dress" look was made for you.

Demeter – Triangle

Smaller shoulders and wider hips.

This is the womanly shape painted by Reuben. In other times, this was the most desired shape because it indicated a pregnancy-friendly body. The challenge for Demeter, and there are lots of Demeters, is to balance the look. Collect a variety of shoulder pads. A Demeter friend used to say that she had, "an hour glass figure and most of the sand was in the bottom!"

Famous Demeters:

Hilary Clinton

Oprah Winfrey

Cokie Roberts

Maya Angelou

Suzanne Pleschette

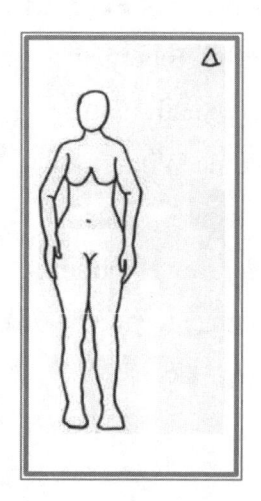

Demeter will be flattered by:

- Softer fabrics and fuller jacket shapes with padded shoulders.
- Larger lapel pins worn high towards the outer edge of the lapel to visually widen the shoulder or short necklaces to keep the attention high on the chest.
- Tapered skirts and slacks that are narrower at the bottom.
- Shorter jackets, if your hips are straight on the sides.
- Mid length jackets if hips are rounded on the sides, never ending at widest part of hip.

Unlocking The Secrets of Successful Women in Business

🗝 Matching top and bottom with contrasting color for blouse, shell, or sweater or scarf to bring attention *up* towards your face and shoulders.

🗝 Lighter colored top, darker bottom.

🗝 Shoulder pads will help balance your figure. *Avoid anything that makes your shoulders look smaller.*

**Because man and woman are the complement of one another, we need woman's thought in national affairs to make a safe and stable government.
Elizabeth Cady Stanton**

Antemis - Inverted Triangle

Wider shoulders, smaller hips.

Artemis has an athletic body that looks wonderful in sporty clothes and can easily project power. She'll probably need to pull shoulder pads out of some clothes, but use caution because that can ruin the line.

Famous Antemises:

Linda Evans

Courtney Love

Princess Diana

Raquel Welch

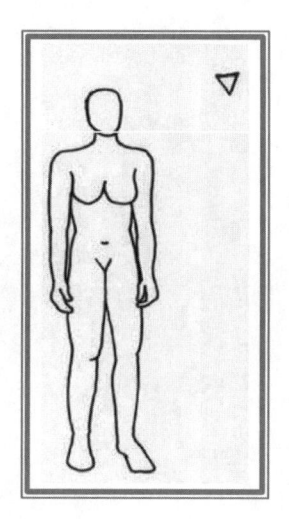

Antemis will be flattered by:

- Suits and dresses with fuller skirt for balance.
- Man-tailored suits.
- Jackets longer and fuller around the hip area.
- Average to full-leg pants.
- Dark on top, light on bottom.
- Longer necklace to pull eye down from the shoulders.
- Lapel pins worn four to six inches, (a hand-width) below the shoulder.

Unlocking The Secrets of Successful Women in Business

Hestia - The Apple

Has a definite tummy, often has great legs. This is *not* the typical after-thirty tummy; it is more pronounced than that. Often it is still visible even at your lowest weight and may be a genetic trait.

Philosophy first: Linda's mother and mother-in-law are both Hestia's with *very* pronounced tummies, and she often helps them choose clothes. Finally, after years of frustration for all involved, Linda had an AHA*!* They both had exactly the same problems — *figure-wise* — as pregnant women. While that may not be a flattering *thought*, if one thinks of the principles involved in maternity clothes, one can flatter the figure. The clothes are designed to give extra room for the tummy, yet the shoulders aren't huge. PS: Pregnancy girdles are *wonderful*! They support the tummy and both moms are so much more comfortable since we figured that out.

Famous Hestias:

Rosie O'Donnell

Roseann Barr

Barbara Bush

Madelaine Albright

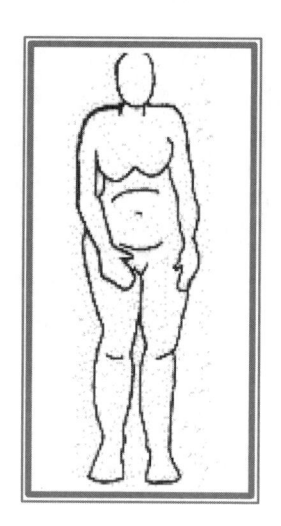

Hestia will be flattered by:

🗝 Softer fabrics with emphasis on the vertical line such as "princess" seaming.

🗝 Longer tops, over-blouses and jackets but no longer than finger tip.

🗝 Skirts no shorter than knee-length. Straight skirts often need alteration to hang well.

🗝 Tucked in scarves and blouses for close-to-the-face accent and contrast.

🗝 One color top and bottom.

🗝 Patterns to create vertical (up and down) lines.

🗝 Some "chemises" and A-line dresses.

> Men, their rights and nothing more.
> Women, their rights and nothing less.
> Susan B. Anthony

Unlocking The Secrets of Successful Women in Business

The Average Body

Hips and shoulders about the same size; waist about a fourth smaller. In a doll that would be 12-9-12. All dresses, suits and pants fit easily whether you are a size 4 or 24. Clothing is fashioned for you, but few women actually have this shape

Be careful not to get carried away. When everything fits well, it is more difficult to establish a clear style and image. What message are you trying to send?

Famous Average Bodies:

Candace Bergen

Barbara Walters

Demi Moore

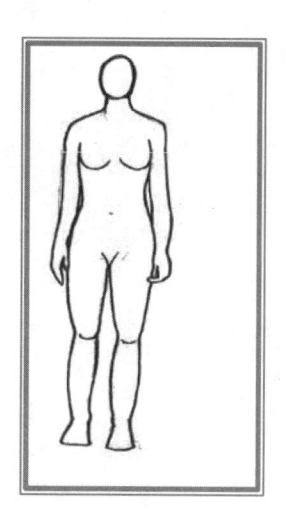

The average body will be flattered by:

🔑 *Just about anything!*

> If we mean to have heroes,
> statesmen and philosophers,
> we should have learned women.
> Abigail Adams

Linda Brakeall and Anna Wildermuth

Just for you . . .

List 3 new ways to flatter your shape.

1.

2.

3.

What do you need to STOP wearing in order to flatter your figure?

What inspirations or insights did you get from this chapter?

What else do you need to know? We might be able to help.
Email us.   anna@personalimagesinc.com
              Linda@LindaBrakeall.com

> Not out of right practice comes right thinking,
> but out of right thinking comes right practice.
> It matters enormously what you think.
> If you think falsely, you will act mistakenly;
> if you think basely,
> your conduct will suit your thinking.
> Annie Besant

Unlocking The Secrets of Successful Women in Business

Key 15

Working With Your Shape And Finding Your Size

Most Of Us Want Someone Else's Shape.

The truth of the matter is that your shape is genetically programmed. You can modify your shape by exercise and diet, but that won't get you longer legs! *Of course you will eat well and get regular exercise anyway because you know that fit, strong and healthy is another key to success.* If you want to modify your natural shape and are willing to work at it all your life, see a nutritionist and get on a prescribed diligent exercise program.

Or you can accept your shape. *Love that body*! *It's yours*! Enhance the best features of your body; minimize the rest. A Leo Burnett marketing study in 1998 reported that most African-American women feel better about their bodies than other women, because they didn't grow up wanting to look like a Barbie doll.

Linda Brakeall and Anna Wildermuth

Real women simply are <u>not</u> shaped like Barbie-Dolls with breasts, legs, hips and waists made by Mattel.

Adjust Your Attitude!

How you feel inside *about your outside* shows. It does not matter if you are 5'8" or 4'8," a size 2 or a size 22. What really matters is how you proportion yourself to the eye and how you feel about it. Most women use a less-than-perfect body as an excuse not to look the best they can. The most common excuses say, *I'm <u>too</u> short, tall, busty, flat-chested, short-legged, long-legged, or fat.* Well, get over it! *Lose the "f" word!* You can appear to have a well-proportioned figure by carefully choosing your clothes. The key is to accept your body, enhance your assets and camouflage the weaker aspects of your shape.

Color, line, design and fit can make you look ten pounds thinner, three inches taller or even a bit shorter.

I rule my looks.
My looks do not rule me.
(On large women vs. the perfect size 6)
Delta Burke

Keys To Shape-Flattering

🗝 **Proper fit** flatters your body and lets your clothes hang better. An inexpensive outfit will look expensive, if it fits well. With alterations anything can be made to look custom fitted so spend the extra money for alterations. Always have room in your clothes to breathe, to move easily and to feel comfortable. However, if your clothes are too big, they will feel sloppy and so will you.

🗝 **Styles and lengths** change, but they can be modified to flatter you. Sometimes one inch shorter or longer is the difference between "sharp" and "frumpy."

🗝 **Direct the eye only where you want attention.** If a jacket ends at the waist, or the fullest part of the hip, the eye will go there. If a necklace ends at the collarbone, or rests on the bust, the eye will go there.

🗝 **Sleeve lengths determine your body proportions.** For average length arms, sleeve length needs to be one inch longer than your wrist. Find an alteration person with a great eye for proportion.

> **To make your arms look longer:** Avoid cuffed sleeves, French cuffed shirts, or accents on sleeves. Raglan sleeves extend the arm. Always have your sleeves altered to hang slightly above the middle of your palm.

> **To make your arms look shorter:** Wear French cuffs on shirts or cuffed sleeved jackets to breakup arm length. Sleeves cover your wrists and showing a little shirtsleeve past the jacket sleeve also visually shortens the arm.

🗝 **Lovely, long legs may appear to have a short torso.** When your jacket covers your hips, and has vertical lines, it visually lengthens your torso.

Linda Brakeall and Anna Wildermuth

To minimize your bust:

🗝 Wear a suit or dress with simple lines and a jacket in the same color.

🗝 Keep jewelry close to the face; a necklace or pin near the collarbone, toward the center to draw attention up and away from bosom. If you wear scarves, tuck them inside your jacket.

🗝 Your "bust point" should hit mid-way between your shoulder and elbow, any lower than that, and you'll look matronly.

🗝 Wear a well-made minimizer bra; probably underwired.

To maximize your bust:

🗝 Wear fitted tops in textured knits, and dramatic tops with styled collars.

🗝 To broaden the bust line, wear lapel pins a hands-length down from shoulder.

🗝 Flowing scarves add color and emphasis to bust.

🗝 Structured clothing adds shape to your bust line and padded bras may help some clothes fit better. **Why not?** *Don't you wear shoulder pads to make clothes fit better?*

> *Rumor has it that*
> *97.3% of the female population*
> *want to look taller and slimmer.*

> You can't treat anyone better
> than you treat yourself.
> Lou Tice

Appearing Taller And Slimmer Is More About Proportion Than Size.

🗝 **Stick with one color top and bottom.** Avoid prints in skirts, pants, dresses and jackets.

🗝 **Skirt lengths hover near your knee.** Much shorter makes it difficult to maintain professional decorum when you are seated and much longer looks frumpy. The next flattering length is mid-calf with matching hose and shoes to lengthen the line.

🗝 **Shoes match the color of clothing closest to shoes**, such as brown shoes with brown pants.

🗝 **Darker hose minimizes fuller legs.** Lighter hose calls attention to legs and white hose belong only in the medical profession.

🗝 **Single-breasted**, one to three button jackets with skirts or slacks in the same color make you look taller and slimmer. A single-breasted coatdress is slimming because the eyes are drawn to the vertical line of buttons. *Double-breasted jackets visually shorten and widen your body.*

🗝 **Shorter jackets if you're less than 5'4" or so.** If you are fuller figured make sure the jacket falls below your waist line but not directly on the widest part of your hip and never longer than fingertips.

🗝 **Unless your shape is rectangular**, wear jackets with some shaping through the waist.

🗝 Average height, 5'4" or so, and above will find a longer jacket with tapered pants and a belt in the same color makes the body look longer.

🗝 **In general, jackets lengths** are most flattering somewhere near your wrist and seldom longer than fingertips.

🗝 **Narrow sleeves and narrow pants legs** make you look longer and thinner. Less bulk in the sleeves and pants equals less visual bulk on you. Avoid bell-bottom trousers unless you want to look like *you* have a bell-bottom!

- **Fine, lighter weight wools, silks, and gabardines** are less bulky and make you look slimmer. Soft fabrics cling, stiffer fabrics don't. If you're trying to camouflage a body part, wear a stiffer fabric.
- **Wear lapel pins high and narrow**, closer to the collarbone.
- **A tucked-in scarf** adds color without bulk.
- **Shoulder pads and padded bras** balance a generous bottom.

Living with integrity means:
Not settling for less than what you know you deserve
in your relationships.
Asking for what you want and need from others.
Speaking your truth,
even though it might create conflict or tension.
Behaving in ways that are in harmony
with your personal values.
Making choices based on what you believe,
and not what others believe.
Barbara DeAngelis

Unlocking The Secrets of Successful Women in Business

If You Are Very Tall And Thin Or If You Want To Look Heavier

Choose:

🔑 Well-fitted clothing. Oversized clothes make you look thinner or sloppy. Clothes that are too tight really show bones or bulges.

🔑 Double breasted jackets. (Who knew they made you look bigger?)

Double-breasted coatdress visually widens the figure.

🔑 Suits with 3/4 length jackets.

🔑 Fuller cut pants.

🔑 Fuller cut sleeves and wide cuffs.

🔑 Vests. (Usually a disaster on busty women.)

🔑 Cuffed pants.

🔑 Longer, fuller skirts.

🔑 Light color stockings.

🔑 Break up the continuous look with two colors or a patterned jacket with a solid skirt or solid pants.

🔑 Belts in contrasting color call attention to tiny waists.

🔑 Wear textured knit dresses or suits, fuller skirts, or bulky fabrics. Bulky fabrics like heavy wools, chenilles and corduroys add bulk to your body.

🔑 You can handle the "layered look," scarves and bold jewelry but *not all at one time.*

Linda Brakeall and Anna Wildermuth

For All Body Shapes, The Key Areas For A Perfect Fit Are:

- From the underarm to waist.
- From the waist to the top of knee.
- Smooth across shoulders, front and back.
- Shoulder width.
- Jacket through waist.
- Crotch length for pants.
- Bust: Choose garments with darts and shaping rather than a "boxy," or a Tee-shirt look if you're a C cup or more.
- Waist.
- Hips.
- Body type and height dictate correct lengths and shapes of:
    Sleeves.
    Pants.
    Jackets.
    Skirts.

*The way I was taught, being black was a plus, always.
Being a human being, being in America,
and being black, all three
were the greatest things that could happen to you.
The combination was unbeatable.*
Leontyne Price

Sizing Has Changed!

Unlike roses, a size is not a size is not a size. You may be looking less than your best merely because you're still buying the same size you always bought. When you have some spare time, try on various sizes and see if another size, or another brand, fits better than what you've been buying. PS: This is another spot where a "personal shopper" could be a time and money-saving asset.

Don't let the size tag be a fit indicator until you have found a brand that always fits. Anna (with 36-inch hips) has an outfit that fits her well in a size 16! There Are Petites, Juniors, Talls, Womans', Woman's Petites, Plus Sizes and Misses Sizes. It is also a trade secret that the more your pay for your clothes, the smaller size you'll wear. So you might be a size 10 in a Dana Buchman and a size 16 at K-Mart. Shop around till you find the best fit. And don't assume that just because the skirt in a given brand fits you well, that the pants will too. Unfortunately, there seems to be little consistency even within a brand.

Try www.therightsize.com for some innovations in fitting. It is a brand new site so we have no first hand information for you, but the concept is that they do a body scan in a cooperating store, in their "Best Fit Pavillion." They'll give you a card that will help you discover which brands will work best on your body! If you try it, let us know how it works.

> Life consists not in holding good cards
> but in playing those you hold well.
> Josh Billings

Linda Brakeall and Anna Wildermuth

Petites and Juniors

Petite sizes are designed for those 5'4" or shorter, also for those who have shorter arms and legs. If you are less than 5'3" - 4," the biggest challenge is getting a good fit from the shoulder to waist. Petite jackets, pants and skirts are an inch or so shorter than for Misses and women's. Most labels have a Petite line, sizes from 0 to 16 P, and J.C. Penny's Misses Petites go up to size 20, though there are fewer choices than you'll find in Misses.

This single-breasted coatdress guides the eye up and down to make a petite look taller and slimmer.

Petite sizes are about ½ inch smaller than Misses in bust, waist and hip. No change in women's sizes, Talbot's has separates in Petites, Average and for the large woman. You can mix and match your jacket, skirt and slacks to create a suit for yourself. Stay with solids — you're not tall enough for any visual clutter. PS: Linda is almost 5'6' but finds that Petites often fit far better than Misses. Go figure!

Juniors sizes tend to be styled for the younger buyer, but sometimes they are the only ones that fit. In that case, choose carefully to look like an adult. The challenge in Juniors is to find clothes that project a serious business look. Avoid "cutesy" fashion.

Nobody holds a good opinion of a person
who a low opinion of self.
Anthony Trollop

Misses

If you are 5'4" to 5'6," you probably will wear "Misses." There are so many choices that it is easy to get careless. Be sure clothes fit your body type. If sleeves or pants are too long, try Petites. If sleeves or pants are too short, try Talls. If the cut is not generous enough, try Woman's or Woman's plus. Small youthful figures might find that Junior tops and sweaters fit better than Misses.

Talls

If you are 5'6" or taller, try Talls. Anna says: "I remember as a child wishing I was shorter, now I feel blessed at 5'8." I can wear almost everything."

Wear monochromatic colors for more power and to accentuate your height. Or you may choose a softer, more approachable look with complementary colors, mix and match fabric textures and colors, unless you want to intimidate — and sometimes you do! You can effectively wear large, dramatic accessories. Avoid flowing fabrics, except for eveningwear. Be sure your jackets, sleeves, skirt hems and pants are long enough and that you have enough room in the shoulders. Snug shoulders will make you look like a grown-up wearing a child's clothes.

Basic Size Chart

	Small		Medium		Large		XL	
	6	8	10	12	14	16	18	20
Bust	34	36	38	40	42	44	46	48
Waist	26	28	30	32	34	36	38	40
Hips	36	38	40	42	44	46	48	50

Petite sizes are ½ inch smaller in bust, waist and hips than Misses, and scaled for 5' 3" or 4" and under, depending on brand.

Junior sizes are similar to regular sizes but shorter from shoulder to waist.

Tall sizes are scaled for those over 5'6" inches tall, same measurements.

Plus size/ Woman's plus sizes are slightly fuller versions of women's sizes.

Woman's sizes, 5'4" and over

	14W	16W	18W	20W	22W	24W	26W	28W
Bust	40	42	44	46	48	50	52	54
Waist	30	32	34	36	38	40	42	44
Hip	41	43	45	47	49	51	53	55
	1x	----------2x----		------3x-----------		4x------		

The Plus Petite

- 45% of female population – Plus and NonPlus – are Petites.
- Most Plus Petites are 5"4" and under.
- Bust sizes, waist and hips sizes are the same as in Woman's sizes.
- Plus Petite sizes: Hip measurement is 7, not 8 inches, below the waist; sleeve is about an inch shorter, shoulder width about 1 1/2 inches less, etc.

Unlocking The Secrets of Successful Women in Business

Just for you . . .

What inspirations or insights did you get from this chapter?

What else do you need to know? We might be able to help.
Email us. anna@personalimagesinc.com
          Linda@LindaBrakeall.com

**Thirty-five is when you finally get your head
together and your body starts falling apart.
Caryn Leschen**

Linda Brakeall and Anna Wildermuth
Key 16

Professional Makeup, Hair And Grooming

Makeup

Once every two years reassess yourself with the help of a makeup artist and hair designer. For the most up to date look, go to the best department store in town for a makeover. Learn what they do and how to do it yourself. It will be time and money well spent.

The best book we've read on makeup is <u>Faces</u> by Kevin Aucoin, (pronounced O'Kwan). Read it thoroughly. It will give you techniques on basic application plus all kinds of camouflage ideas. His best points: You seldom need to buy single-use items. A lipliner can be an eyeliner if the color is right, and blush can be lipstick and vice versa. And he also said that price alone does not indicate quality. That's nice to know.

Buy a sample size when possible, or use the tester in the store, and wear it for several hours to see if the color remains true and the makeup stays on. You want to do your makeup in the morning and still look presentable when you go home. Who has time to primp all day long?

Makeup that dates you:

Too much makeup, or none at all, is the first sign that you're not "with it." Pink and coral toned lipsticks are too soft to go with today's fashions. Orange-based foundation should be replaced immediately, and any lipliner that is not blended with your lipstick, especially brown, makes you look like a refugee from the sixties.

Watch TV network news anchorwomen to see what is current.

Networks invest a lot of money to make sure those women look up-to-date. If network anchorwomen are wearing big sooty, dark-lined eyes like Sophia Loren did in her movies from the 1960's, and piles of stiff hair, then you may feel free to do so. Otherwise, today's look is far more natural.

Miscellaneous make up thoughts

- Makeup should not be kept more than one year after it has been opened. Eye makeup should be discarded after six months because bacteria grow there.
- Lipliner is a wonderful asset to gently define the mouth but keep it on the line of the lip or just ever so slightly within or beyond the lip. Let Kevin Aucoin or someone like him reconstruct lip lines. Most of us civilians do a very poor job of

it. And the mouth that you were trying to improve looks like a personal urban renewal project gone astray!

- Lipstick will stay put if you put concealer or a makeup base on lips, line with a pencil that is close in color to your lipstick. (You can line before or after applying lipstick. Try it both ways and see which is better on you.) Fill in with lipstick and gently blot. Powder and repeat the whole process. Your lipstick will stay in place perfectly for 4 - 8 hours, even through lunch.

- Be careful if you mix lipstick colors because the bases may not be compatible and the color may change after application.

- The purpose of eyeliner is to make your eyelashes look longer, not to draw lines on your eyelids! There should be no discernable "line." Blend, blend, blend!

Psst!
Have you noticed that after 40, it takes longer and longer to get that natural look?

I've come to trust that not all events
will unfold exactly as I want
but that I will be fine either way.
Marianne Williamson

Professional Hair

From Across The Room, Your Hairstyle Can Date You.

"To keep abreast of what is going on observe, observe, observe… in magazines, movies and on television," says Ginger and Verna, hair designers from A Shear Encounter Salon.

Think simple and elegant, not fussy.

Your hair says a lot about how you perceive yourself and how you take care of yourself. If it is straggly and has obvious roots showing, the message you send to the rest of the world is: "Who cares?" It is a very obvious part of the total package that you present.

Again, check out those TV news anchorwomen. Watch how the new local weather "girls" have "busy" and longer hair. As they get promoted, the hair tends to be sleeker and shorter. Remember Melanie Griffith in "Working Girl?" The long fussy hair went first. *"I need serious hair!"* Then she got some elegant clothes, *and then she got Harrison Ford* by the end of the movie. Need we say more?

After the age of 25, professional women rarely wear their hair past shoulder length. If it is longer than that, it is worn up. Mature women with hair hanging past their shoulders look older, not younger! Besides emphasizing lines and wrinkles, longer hair sends a message that says: "I think of myself as a sexy woman first." Nothing wrong with that, unless you want to be chairman of the board, or get a promotion. They should be thinking of you as a competent professional first, and a woman second.

Wash your hair often enough so that it always looks, feels and smells wonderful. If you have dry hair that may only be two or three times a week. For many, it is part of the daily routine. Experiment and find out what works best for you and your hair.

UNIVERSITY STUDY CONCLUDES HAIRSTYLES MAKE OR BREAK YOUR FIRST IMPRESSION

Evidence Reveals Different Hairstyles Are Linked To Perceived Personality Traits

New Haven, CT, February 21, 2001 - Within three seconds of meeting you, people form a first impression about the type of person you are, and it's not your face that gives you away - it's your hairstyle! **A recent study validates that your hairstyle dictates the first impression you make, significantly overpowering the impact of facial features.**

We all know how important it is to make a good first impression, whether you're looking for a new job, getting ready for a first date, or meeting the potential in-laws. **Your choice of hairstyle might project an image of intelligence and self-assurance, or one of insecurity and conceit, so make your style work for you**.

Dr. Marianne LaFrance, director of the study First Impressions and Hair Impressions and Professor of Psychology and Professor of Women's and Gender Studies at Yale University, asserts that until now there has been no investigation of the unique effect hairstyle has on first impressions.

> "We wanted to learn whether the frame around the face - the hairstyle - can significantly alter how a person is seen," says Dr. LaFrance. "We found that different hairstyles quickly lead others to 'see' different kinds of people."

> Read more about this at www.physique.com

Miscellaneous Hair Tips:

🔑 Avoid extremes of color or style. Too long, too short, too blonde, too dark, too straight, or too curly does not send a professional message.

🔑 If your hair color requires only a single process (as opposed to taking the color out and then putting new color in), you can probably do it yourself. Many of the new hair coloring products actually improve your hair by giving it more body.

🔑 Plan on color touch-ups every three to four weeks. If your hair grows quickly, you may have to touch up your roots as often as every two weeks.

🔑 Hair that is too dark for your skin will add years to your face. As we age, lighter hair is kinder and more flattering. The tone of the color makes the difference. Use a good colorist to find the right shade and make your eyebrows match your hair.

🔑 Graying hair will add years to your face. If you like it gray, or choose not to color, use a rinse to add shine and prevent yellowing.

🔑 Shiny hair looks healthy and youthful! Use a shine spray for thin, fine hair and for thick hair a shine gel. Those with fine, straight hair may require a body perm every three to four months to keep an easy care style that looks well cared for and smart.

> The most exhausting thing
> in life is being insincere.
> Anne Morrow Lindbergh

Linda Brakeall and Anna Wildermuth

Professional Grooming And Hygiene

Teeth

It is important that your teeth look as good today as when you turned 21. If tea, coffee or cigarettes have stained your teeth, see your dentist. She/he may recommend teeth whiteners.

Breath

Bad breath causes people to distance themselves from you. Check with your dentist first if you have a chronic problem. Always carry breath mints and fresheners; drops are less conspicuous than sprays. Brush if possible after each meal. Stay away from garlic and onions during workday lunch and dinners.

Note: Talking a lot dries out the mouth and a dry mouth causes bad breath. Sip water and keep those mints handy during meetings.

Hands and Cuticles

Nails that project a professional look are lightly colored and fairly short and shaped slightly rounded. It is important to keep you hands and cuticles soft and free of hangnails. Give yourself or get a manicure every 7-14 days. Stay away from overly long and bright colored nails, which are distracting.

Tip: Professional manicurist Allison says: "Vitamin E oil on your cuticles morning and night really helps your hands look like a model's."

Body Hair

No facial hair, underarm hair or hair on your legs. Try cream depilatories like Nair, or waxing to avoid shaving. Eyebrows are natural and plucked or waxed into shape, *not* shaved off and then penciled in.

> You know, the hardest thing about having
> cerebral palsy and being a woman?
> It's plucking your eyebrows.
> That's how I originally got pierced ears!
> Geri Jewell

Perfume And Smoke In The Workplace

So many people are allergic to everything these days that you may choose to avoid smoking and wearing perfume in the office environment. Wear unscented *everything* such as deodorant, hair products, hand cream, and sun screen to prevent aroma and allergy conflicts.

Perfume should be subtle, not overwhelming. If someone shakes your hand, they may notice your perfume. They shouldn't notice if you just walk by. Keep perfume and cologne in the refrigerator. It deteriorates within a year when opened and exposed to light and heat. You may not notice it when you put it on but after awhile, it will smell different. *And not in a good way!*

Smoking is a no-no even at a dinner when your client smokes. We do not recommend smoking in public unless you know everyone very well. And watch where the smoke goes.

Linda Brakeall and Anna Wildermuth

5 Keys To Smart Grooming:

1. Current hairstyle.
2. Every two years, review and renew your makeup.
3. Fresh breath and clean teeth.
4. Well-manicured nails and hands.
5. Subtle, signature cologne.

I refuse to think of them as chin hairs.
I think of them as stray eyebrows.
Janette Barber

My second favorite household chore is ironing.
My first being hitting my head
on the top bunk bed until I faint.
Erma Bombeck

I try to take one day at a time,
but sometimes several days attack me at once.
Jennifer Unlimited

Unlocking The Secrets of Successful Women in Business

Just for you . . .

List 3 or more action steps to update your makeup, hair and grooming.

1.

2.

3.

What do you need to STOP doing in order for your hair, makeup and grooming to be smart and current?

What inspirations or insights did you get from this chapter?

> We make a living by what we get,
> but we make a life by what we give.
> Winston Churchill"

> If you can spend a perfectly useless afternoon
> in a perfectly useless manner,
> you have learned how to live.
> Lin Yutang

Linda Brakeall and Anna Wildermuth
Key 17

Business Etiquette and Professional Grace

Etiquette or "doing the right thing" should always be based on kindness and caring for people's needs. You are acting in their interests, not your own, and your kindness stems from thoughtfulness and consideration. It involves far more than selecting the correct fork at a fancy dinner.

What **to do often involves proper protocol and it is important to know what is expected of you in any situation.** *How* to do it, on the other hand, involves your personal style and what I (Anna) call *professional grace*.

> "If you are never scared, embarrassed or hurt, it means you never take chances."
> Julia Soul

Professional Grace

The definition of grace is "ease and suppleness of movement or bearing." It is one's ability to oil the wheels, to take care of people, to manage situations and generally walk toward the clearings in life. Grace requires acute intuitive qualities, which include doing or saying the right thing at the right time, thinking on your feet, flexibility, consideration of people's needs, and listening to the said and the unsaid. It also requires finding simple, elegant solutions that allow things to be accomplished without assigning blame and with absolute integrity. There are lots of books available to specifically guide you in detail but we'd like to review the highlights for you.

Professional grace and good etiquette requires that you not call attention to the mistakes of others.

Remember Names!

If etiquette is based on kindness, one of the kindest things you can do is remember the names of people you meet. Use their names frequently. People love it because it makes them feel important.

The summer we were writing this book, Linda ran into an Illinois State Legislator, Kay Wojcik, at a minor league baseball game. The legislator, whom Linda had met a number of times, but not in recent history, obviously remembered Linda. Linda could tell by the warmth and sincerity of her greeting. "Why hello. It is so good to see *you*. It's been ages!" Linda knew that *she* was remembered but really didn't expect the Congresswoman to remember her name. It *had* been years! During the conversation, maybe five minutes later, Kay used her name. Now, we all know that Kay was groping frantically for five minutes to find it, as would we all. And Linda didn't really expect her to remember it, but it still made a positive impression.

Some people have a knack for remembering names. Some take courses and learn how to do it by mnemonic tricks, or by association.

> *Some individuals are simply so warm*
> *and gracious that no one minds*
> *if one's name is forgotten.*

4 Keys To Remembering Names:

1. **Write names down if you are on the phone**. The dullest pencil is better than the sharpest memory. (Am I the only one who has forgotten names mid-sentence?) On the phone, you can write it and read it.

2. **Use double-think** (often called associations), to remember when introduced such as: Bill is wearing a blue tie. B for blue, B for Bill. *Bill Blue Tie.* Got it.

3. **If you forget, ask them immediately.** "Forgive me. I don't think I really heard your name when we were introduced. I'm Anna Wildermuth and you are . . ." If you forget again, listen for someone else to mention it or ask the host. Or, "Your name has momentarily slipped my mind."

4. **For the person who looks familiar:** " I always remember great faces like yours, but you'll have to help me with your name. I'm Anna Wildermuth and you are... "

Success is the ability to pursue one's own goals.
Margaret Mead

Unlocking The Secrets of Successful Women in Business

The Professional Handshake

This initial physical contact sets the tone of the beginning of your relationship. In general, men tend to be better at firm handshakes than women; probably because they've had more practice. The correct professional handshake is firm, palm to palm, the net of the skin between the index finger and the thumb going all the way to meet the same place on the hand of the person you are meeting.

Men tend to shake hands ever-so-delicately with women. I suspect they are trying to be gentle, not patronizing. But every time we let that happen, it sends a subliminal message that there is a *reason* why they must be gentle; because we're *girls*, not grown women who won't break and can handle themselves quite well, thank you very much.

> *So next time they delicately grasp your finger-tips, slip your hand all the way into theirs and shake hands firmly. If they look shocked, smile. They'll get over it!*

Speaking of smiles, a warm smile is the first step to establishing a warm relationship. Some people who are thinking intensely will frown, not because they are unhappy or angry, merely because they are thinking. Ask your friends if you do that. If you seldom smile, you may look unfriendly and if you frown all the time, the message is clear: You're not a lot of fun. You may be sending messages that you didn't plan to send but you can modify that behavior. Smiling is a habit as well as a natural inclination. We don't want you to smile *all* the time and look like the village idiot, but *most of the time* it's an asset.

Linda Brakeall and Anna Wildermuth

How Much Is Enough Personal Space?

This is different for different people but the general rule in North America is about an arm's length. If your own personal space is smaller or larger than that, you may find that people feel crowded or distant when they are with you. Try to adjust. If others crowd you or are too distant for your own personal comfort, be aware and think, "Isn't that interesting?" Whenever you can work with *their* space requirements, they'll be more comfortable.

Business Etiquette 2001 Or Traditional Etiquette?
Guest Columnist Gloria Peterson, Global Protocol

There seem to be before 5:00 p.m. and after 5:00 p.m. rules. Do you find approaching a car with a male business colleague or client creates an awkward moment? For example, before 5:00 p.m., a businesswoman prefers to open her own door, but after 5:00 p.m., she expects the gentleman to open her door. Right?

The equal-opportunity movement was fostered in great part by the feminist movement of the 1960s and 1970s. It has created two sets of rules: One for business and one for social situations. This can certainly create misinterpretations and confusion.

Caution: Our business-related, unisex, gender rules may not apply in other countries. When in doubt, follow the traditional social rules. The modern work environment prefers that men and women be treated equally as professionals. However, in some regions (and countries), the traditional rule still dominates.

For example, modern business etiquette dictates:

1. The use of "Ms." when addressing businesswomen, except when informed otherwise or in a social situation.

The use of "Ms." grew during the feminist movement of the 1970s and with the introduction of Gloria Steinem's magazine entitled "*Ms*." Privacy regarding a Woman's marital status became important. Controversy continued regarding the use of "Ms" throughout the 1970s and 1980s; however, since the 1990s, "Ms." is the accepted honorific for businesswomen.

The title, Mr., does not offer any information to marital status. Consequently, women in business selected the title, "Ms." to keep their marital status private.

Traditional etiquette accepts the title of Mrs.

2. Handshakes. This has caused many an awkward moment for men who were taught to always to wait for women to initiate a handshake. Women who are not aware of this rule are often offended when a handshake is not offered.

Traditional etiquette dictates that it would be considered bad form for a man to initiate a handshake to a woman. This rule is still observed in most countries other than the US.

3. Both genders stand when being greeted or introduced to show respect.

Traditional etiquette allows the woman to remain seated during introductions.

4. Opening doors and help with coats should be treated as a courtesy and not gender-related. It is polite for either the man or woman to extend this courtesy.

Traditional etiquette dictates that a man should always open the door for a woman and help her with her wrap.

Business etiquette today is based on professional hierarchy unlike social etiquette, which is based on gender. No one should be given special treatment in the business arena because of gender. However, a courtesy is always welcome and should be accepted gracefully.

It is equally important for a businesswoman to accept an act of good form as a courtesy and simply say, "Thank you," and not interpret this courtesy as patronizing or preferential treatment.

Following the rules of etiquette is not about following rigid rules. It is about using common sense and adjusting behavior to fit the situation.

Reprinted with permission by Gloria Petersen, President, Global Protocol, Inc. www.globalprotocol.com, Gpetersen@Globalprotocol.com.

Linda Brakeall and Anna Wildermuth

Introduction Etiquette

General Rule:
Say the most important person's name first. Gender is not a factor.

🔑 Say the older person's name first, when both are in comparable positions.

🔑 Say the senior executive's name first when introducing him or her to a junior executive.

🔑 Always state the higher-ranking person's name first even if he or she is younger.

🔑 Say a client or customer's name first when introducing him/her to one of your company executives.

🔑 Say the official person's name first when introducing him/her to a non-official person.

🔑 Say the name of the higher-ranking person, (senior executive, other company executive, client or official) followed by the name of the other individual.

🔑 Official titles are used for public and government officials even after they left office or retired as courtesy and expression of respect.

Examples:
Junior to senior executive:
"Senior Executive, I would like to introduce Junior Executive."

Client to your company's senior executive:
(The client is the most important person.)
"Carol Richards, I'd like you to meet Paula Camembert, who is the Vice President of our company.

Add a follow-up line to connect the two so they can converse intelligently on a common topic. "Paula, Ms. Richards' company is our newest client and distributes electrical products."

Unlocking The Secrets of Successful Women in Business

Client to a group:
"Carol, I would like to introduce my colleagues from XYZ Enterprises: Frank Morgan, Paula Camembert and John Jacobs. This is Carol Richards, President of DEF, an electrical distribution company who is our newest client."

Keys to successful introductions:

1. Avoid using nicknames unless that name is the person's business name such as Jimmy Carter.
2. Use first and last names; repeat name of person in conversation.
3. Speak clearly and slowly so each name can be heard.
4. Introductions should always include information that will be of interest to both parties and help start conversation between the two, perhaps a brief statement about each person's interests or recent accomplishments.

*Resource: <u>Power Etiquette: What You Don't Know Can Kill Your Career</u>

> You are your own best laboratory.
> Observe what goes on within you.
> You are a microcosm of the world.
> Linda Brakeall

Linda Brakeall and Anna Wildermuth

Dining Etiquette

Many thirty-somethings on the corporate fast-track are taking courses on "corporate dining." While it may sound silly, it is often necessary in today's practically Emily Post-free world! If you said, "Who's she?" that confirms our premise. I'm (Anna) frequently called into major corporations to cover the etiquette basics because it is so seldom taught at home.

We can all become poised, informed and charming dining companions by knowing the rules, most of which are based on common sense, and avoiding the most obvious mistakes. Never call attention to the dining mistakes of others or be overly apologetic about your own. **Be calm and cheerful. Mistakes happen. Life goes on.**

> **Flexible people don't get bent out of shape.**
> **Unknown**

Dining Basics

Napkins: Place your napkin on your lap before eating or drinking anything. The waiter may assist you.

Napkin faux pas include flapping your napkin open, putting it on the table before the meal has ended and using it to blow or wipe your nose. Fold your napkin and place it beside your plate at the end of the meal.

Memorize this: Dry to the left, wet to the right. Translation: *Your* bread and salad plates are on your left. Y*our* cup and glasses are on your right. If someone uses your bread plate, wait for a waiter to come by and quietly request another one. (Sometimes, *everyone* uses the wrong bread plate. Chuckle quietly to yourself, no comment is required.)

Most utensils are used from the outside in. If there are several forks, use the one on the outside for the first course and work your way in. Utensils for dessert are often put on the table across the top of the plate, but if you find a fork or spoon next to your plate, that's probably for dessert. If in doubt, watch your host. And if you eat with the wrong fork, it's unlikely anyone will notice or care. Just don't mention it.

Dining experiences will vary. You can handle them with more confidence by remembering the basics: Common courtesy, a positive attitude, and a cheerful demeanor.

Dining Embarrassments

🔑 If you spill something, quickly and quietly blot it with your napkin, and ask the waiter for another napkin.

🔑 If you spill something on someone else, apologize, and offer to pay for the dry cleaning, but let the other person handle the wiping and blotting.

🔑 If you burp, touch your napkin to your lips, and say, "Pardon me," to no one in particular.

*Common sense and courtesy
will keep you from committing most
of these business dining mistakes.*

Don't

🔑 Sit down until everyone has gathered at your table.

🔑 Put purse, keys, gloves, phone etc. on the table.

🔑 Let your phone or pager ring during a meal.

🔑 Begin eating until the guest of honor, senior person, your boss, or your guest, has taken his or her first bite.

🔑 Salt or otherwise season your food before you taste. (The psychoanalysts in the group will assume that you always jump to conclusions.)

🔑 Butter all the bread or roll at once. Tear off bite size pieces and butter a bite or two at a time. Put butter first on your bread plate or dinner plate, not directly on your roll.

🔑 Cut more than one or two bites of meat or anything else, at one time.

🔑 Lean over to reach food. Ask to have it passed to you.

🔑 Dunk your food.

🔑 Speak with your mouth full or chew with your mouth open.

🔑 Crumble crackers in your soup, or blow on any liquid that is too hot.

🔑 Overload your plate at a buffet.

🔑 Hold the knife like a dagger or wrap your whole hand around the fork.

🔑 Put used cutlery back on the table.

🔑 Put elbows on table during the meal.

🔑 Slouch, squirm, or tilt your chair.

🔑 Pick or poke at your teeth.

🔑 Leave lipstick smears on napkins.

🔑 Push your plate away, and don't push your chair back when you have finished eating.

🔑 Smoke at the table.

🔑 Ask people where they are going when they leave the table.

🔑 Ask about medication taken with a meal.

🔑 Finish your meal before or after everyone else.

🔑 Discuss a problem about the check with the waiter at the table.

Unlocking The Secrets of Successful Women in Business

**What happens to you is not as important
as how you react to what happens to you.
Thaddeus Golas**

Finger Foods

The following foods may be eaten with your fingers. An even better idea is to order only easy-to-eat, non-finger foods when you are planning to discuss business so that you can maintain focus. Practice eating *italicized items* on your own before ordering in public. Save fried chicken, ribs, and corn on the cob for picnics. They are difficult to eat neatly.

- Tortillas, bacon, celery, pickles, radishes and olives.

- Shrimp when tails are left on, except shrimp cocktail.

- *Artichokes* - Pull the leaf through your teeth to remove the edible part. When you get to the heart, use a knife to scrape the fuzzy part off, and then use a knife and fork.

- *Oysters* - Hold with one hand, use seafood fork in other.

- *Clams* - Hold with one hand, use seafood fork in other.

- *Snails* - Use metal holders with left hand, use seafood fork with right, or vice versa if you're left-handed.

- *Lobster* - If you order only the lobster tail, you can use a knife and fork.

**Remember the scene in *Pretty Woman*
when Julia Robert's snail shell flew
into the waiter's hand?**

I hate housework!
You make the beds, you do the dishes
– and six months later you have to start all over again.
Joan Rivers

Linda Brakeall and Anna Wildermuth

Keys To Hosting A Business Meal

🔑 If possible, entertain at familiar restaurants where you are known. All surprises are not pleasant!

🔑 "Power breakfasts" are often popular with early birds, those with very full calendars or modest budgets.

🔑 If you're having lunch with a client, consider going early, probably before noon for quick service and after 1 pm if you need an extended time to talk after most of the lunch crowd has departed.

🔑 Dinner is usually the best meal for building serious relationships. No one is in a rush to get back to the office and the pace is easier.

> – During dinner, find out about the person who is your client. What does he or she like to do for fun? What's important to him or her? What are his or her values? Schedule a follow-up meeting at the office or the next day to nail down details or to ask for the order.

> – You may discuss light business after the meal is ordered but don't discuss business during the meal unless the client begins the discussion. Try to save serious business discussions for dessert.

🔑 Allow your client to order a beverage first. Order liquor for yourself only if your client has done so. Enjoy yourself, but use discretion and drink lightly with clients especially when the relationship is new.

🔑 The host or hostess should order last and the host or hostess is responsible for asking the wait staff for water, etc. Obviously, the host or hostess should always pick up the check.

🔑 Never let your client eat alone. You don't have to eat what you don't want but you can nibble at a salad while he or she is eating an appetizer or drink coffee when he or she is having dessert.

Unlocking The Secrets of Successful Women in Business

Just for you . . .

List 3 or more things to improve your business etiquette and professional grace.

1.

2.

3.

What do you need to STOP doing to display more professional grace?

What inspirations or insights did you get from this chapter?

What else do you need to know? We might be able to help.
Email us. anna@personalimagesinc.com
       Linda@LindaBrakeall.com

> There came a time when the risk to remain tight in the bud was more painful than the risk it took to blossom.
> **Anais Nin**

Linda Brakeall and Anna Wildermuth

Key 18

Business Communication Etiquette

Professional Voice Mail

When they call you and you're not there.

Change your voice mail message daily or weekly and keep it to less than thirty seconds. Tell callers your schedule for the day or the week to indicate that your message is current and let callers know when you will be available. Tips or advertisements in your voice mail message are tiresome for repeat callers. *Many of them are tiresome the first time.* Be friendly, concise, and speak slowly. And *smile* while you are recording your message, they'll hear it. You may have to record your message several times to get it right. It's worth the effort.

Unlocking The Secrets of Successful Women in Business

The message you record for your callers should include:

🗝 Your name and the name of your company or division.

🗝 Let callers know when you will be returning calls.

🗝 If appropriate, tell them how to get your fax number, pager or e-mail address; sometimes that's why they called.

🗝 How to contact a human being for urgent matters.

Leaving a voice mail message:

🗝 Speak slowly.

🗝 Give your name and spell it if it's more complicated than Smith.

🗝 Slowly give your phone number twice, once at the beginning and again at the end.

🗝 Tell why you are calling.

🗝 Mention a good time to call you back.

🗝 If you have a request, be sure to tell the person your deadline without leaving an ultimatum. "I'd appreciate hearing from you before my deadline on Friday," is much better for human relations than, "If you don't call me back by Friday, I'll report you to the National Enquirer."

**Find your true calling.
Brian Tracy**

Returning phone calls.

🔑 Always return phone calls within 24 hours or have your assistant do so. You don't want people feeling neglected. If returning the call quickly is impossible, your voice mail message should warn callers of the delay.

🔑 Return all phone calls, even if you cannot help the caller, to show your courtesy and professionalism. To do otherwise is rude. By the way, many long-term relationships start from such a simple act of kindness.

Professional Correspondence

Notes and letters.

Never send anything that is confrontational. It is often impossible to undo damage and hurt feelings caused by a note or letter sent in the heat of anger or frustration. Be sure to spell the person's name and title correctly.

Spell-check and proof read all correspondence before you mail it. Some of a computer's grammar suggestions would make your 8th grade English teacher pull out her hair! All final editing has to be done by you or your assistant.

Computers have spell-check.
They don't have "Idiot Check" and
they don't have "Homonym Check."

Unlocking The Secrets of Successful Women in Business

Tips For Professional Success In Cyberspace

Business E-Mail Is Business Correspondence

Your e-mail has a life of it's own. Remember, someone else can read all e-mail. Use appropriate discretion and assume that all messages could find their way to your boss's computer or make the front page of tomorrow's newspaper.

🔑 Do not send e-mail that is off-color or offensive.

🔑 Consider carefully before sending *any* jokes and keep them clean.

🔑 Save messages you send for at least 30 days; you may need them again.

🔑 File the ones you know are important.

Sending business e-mail messages:

Greeting: Start your message with a greeting such as Hello, Hi, or Dear Xxxx. One of our friends deletes all messages that don't start like that unless it is someone he already knows. He says the lack of courtesy at the beginning of such a message, *from a stranger,* tells him the sender is not a sensitive person and he chooses not to deal with them at all. Not everyone feels like that, but what if your client *does?*

Closure: End the message with Sincerely, Best regards or Thank you, which can be part of your "Signature File." (On the tool bar, look for **Tools**, then **Options,** then you should find **Signatures.)**

Subject matter: Always indicate a specific subject to help the recipient decide which messages to read first, and make it easier to find later.

Attachments: Ask your recipient for preferences regarding attachments. Some recipients may not be able to open attachments in all formats. You may be able to accommodate such recipients by copying the text of your document and including it at the end of your message. Some people choose to do both. Some Internet service providers cannot deal with large files and will reject them. You can solve that problem by sending a large file in pieces numbered Part 1, Part 2, etc., or using a software program such as Zip to compress files.

Forwarding: In forwarding a message, do not share others' e-mail addresses. Delete other addresses from the message.

Cyber-abbreviations: For business correspondence, take off the >>>>> when forwarding messages. Avoid cyberspace shorthand such as LOL, (for Laughing Out Loud) and emoticons (that's a cyber-word) such as : -) and ; - (. They're unprofessional.

Message length: Keep your e-mail as short as possible. This is supposed to be a *fast* way of communicating!

Personal e-mails: Check out your company policy, but "Less is more" is a good rule.

Replying to e-mail messages:

Reply to all e-mail that came from another human being. It is frustrating not to know if your e-mail has been read. The reply can be brief when you include the original e-mail message to provide continuity. If you don't include the original message, you are prolonging the process because it's hard to remember the details of all messages received and sent daily. (Original messages can be included automatically by looking at "Tools" where you'll find either "Preferences" or "Options." Open the tab called "Reply" or "Send." Then look for a place to check mark, "Include original message.")

While some formality is required with clients, customers etc., quick responses like this are often adequate with business friends when the original messages are included:
"Thanks!"
"Will do."
"You'll have it Tuesday"
"See you there."

Respond in the same tone of the sender: If the original e-mail began, "Dear Anna," be sure to begin your note with "Dear Xxxx." If it started, "Hi!" You can do likewise. If it was signed, "Sincerely," echo the form.

Why? Each of us thinks we are "correct." No one says, *"Hmmmm. How can I look really dumb and offend the recipient of this message?"* Whatever form and tone is sent to you is probably comfortable for the sender. If you seem "like them," they'll be more comfortable with you.

Without a face and a voice, it is easy to misunderstand messages.

Take extra care to make sure that the "tone of the message" is the tone you planned to convey. If you're grinning when you write, do this: <grin> so that the recipient hears the tone of the e-mail. Use other similar devices so that you are "heard" correctly.

From Linda: Let the e-mail message get cold for a few minutes before you send it and re-read once more. Does the message still make sense? Many notes, jotted quickly, fail this test. Mine included. I sent a note to another writer about my next book and said: "My next book in the Unlocking The Secrets

Series is...ready? Unlocking The Secrets Of The Weekday WomanWarrior(tm)."

When I said, "Ready?" I was hearing (in my own little head) a drum roll. When I re-read it, it appeared that the book was incomplete. That was not the message I intended! Perhaps I could have said, " My next book in the Unlocking The Secrets series is, (Are you ready for this, Rita? May I have a drum roll, please? Da-dah!) Unlocking The Secrets Of The WeekDay WomanWarrior(tm)." Do you "hear" the difference?

What if you are not "into" e-mail?

Many people for a variety of reasons have an e-mail address but they seldom ever check their e-mail. Or they have an assistant print out the e-mail messages and then reply — by hand — on the hard copy. (I know this happens. I did not make this up!) Then the assistant types the messages and replies to the sender. No wonder they're not "into e-mail." That's laborious!

In any event if you know you will not reply to e-mail within 24 hours, you *must* find a way to notify those who e-mail you. E-mail aficionados expect a response within hours, not days. (In the interest of good customer relations, we are deleting the stern lecture about moving into the 21st century.) The easiest way is to have your assistant, *or your kid,* set up an "auto-responder" for you. Every e-mail that comes into your mailbox will receive an immediate reply. You choose what to say but we'd recommend that you tell your correspondents not to expect an immediate reply and offer your phone number for "quicker response." **As long as people know what to expect, they'll find a way to cope.**

Perhaps this doesn't apply to you, but we have sent (and received) messages that we know would have never been sent if someone had taken just a few more minutes to think it through or cool down. In most e-mail programs, you can adjust "Preferences" so that your mail is not sent immediately. We've found that to be ....*ummmm*... career-enhancing! <smile> ; -)

Miscellaneous Keys To E-Mail:

🗝 "Reply" does not always go to the person who e-mailed you *if the e-mail was forwarded*. Be sure you have the correct return address in the TO box.

🗝 Clear out your e-mail message box at least weekly because it is as distracting as a messy desk. Sort e-mail as you would sort regular mail. Some can be tossed (deleted) immediately, some you glance at and then toss. Some requires action, and some gets filed. **And the best thing about e-mail is that you can retrieve what you deleted until you empty your recycle bin.** And you never get messy digging through the coffee-grounds infested trash.

Just for you . . .

List 3 action steps to improve your business and cyber-communications.

1.

2.

3.

What do you need to STOP doing in order to simplify your business communication?

What inspirations or insights did you get from this chapter?

Linda Brakeall and Anna Wildermuth

Key 19

Interviewing For a New Job

1. Prepare to fit in.
2. Do your homework.
3. Prepare answers.
4. Match your insides to your outside.
5. At the interview or "Show Time!"
6. Bottom line.

Step 1.
Prepare To Fit In

If you haven't already done so, please read the Charm and Charisma chapter. It's designed for the sales situation, but there is no more important sales situation than an interview. **In the first 30 seconds the interviewer has to feel that you would fit in and work out in this position.** Think long and hard about how you can convey that initial impression. Create an exterior image and project an attitude that will blend with the corporate culture of the company you'd like to work for.

I (Linda) say, "create" advisedly. I don't want you to be anything that you are not because that would be dishonest. But you do have a choice about which parts of **you,** you present. And there is nothing wrong with letting them see the parts of you that you are sure they would appreciate *first*. Save some surprises for later.

> Courage is the price that life exacts for granting peace.
> Amelia Earhart

Step 2
Do Your Homework!

Learn as much in advance as you can about how the people in this company think, their vocabulary, their jargon, their educational background and what they are trying to accomplish. Then figure out how you can blend into those surroundings.

Do you know someone who works there who might help you out?

Or worked there previously? This is a wonderful opportunity for networking. A phone call, cup of coffee, or lunch may be a wise investment, if you ask a lot of questions to give you a head start.

Think gossip!

- Ask about people, relationships, and corporate atmosphere.
- Why do people leave? Is there a high turnover rate?

- 🗝 Ask if the employees like and/or know the CEO.
- 🗝 Ask about management style.
- 🗝 Ask about employees: Are they all work? All play? Are they productive?
- 🗝 What's the dress code?
- 🗝 Does it sound like the place/atmosphere/people would suit you?
- 🗝 Ask your friend if he/she thinks you would fit in. If not, why not? And how could you modify whatever that is? If it is only a surface difference, try to adapt. If it is a basic value issue, get out now.

Do your homework and determine if you want to work there.

You want to "mirror" the *image* of a person who would work at this particular company. You want to speak and work at their speed. You want to sort of look like them, sort of sound like them, be likeable and blend in.

Learn as much as possible about the corporate and financial health of any company where you might possibly work.

Check out the 10K and 10Q detail section of their annual report filed with the U.S. Securities and Exchange Commission, which tells you what worries a company about their business. (www.Edgar-online.com, then go to CIK Lookup.) It includes the balance sheet of assets and liabilities, equities, the profit and loss statements plus a lot of details that are usually interesting only to those involved, but may give you a clue about the inner workings.

Unlocking The Secrets of Successful Women in Business

You might also go to the company's website and search for "Annual Report." There will usually be a way to check various sections of that annual report. The financial sections will lead you to "Management Discussions," "Our Future," "Cautions," and similar topics. **Be prepared to skim lots of pages to get a feel for what's going on at a company and follow the trails.** It won't be easy. If it were, everyone would do it!

There is some risk involved in referring to the 10K and 10Q. You could be stepping on tender toes. On the other hand, they will definitely know you've done your homework!

This research may give you background, and the basis for an intelligent conversation or at least you'll know some of the particulars and you'll appear very savvy during your interview. During an interview, a friend of mine said that she had noticed in their annual report that a radical new product was in development. She asked if that would be a potential area of liability for the company.

The interviewer, who happened to be a VP of product development, stopped dead in his tracks looked at her for a long minute, and said, "No one on our executive board has asked that question." At that moment he began to take her seriously.

> If we did all the things we are capable of doing,
> we would literally astound ourselves.
> Thomas Alva Edison

> Failure is impossible.
> Susan B. Anthony

Step 3
Prepare Answers

Figure out all the questions the interviewer might ask you, then figure out the answers and rehearse them!

Role-play with a friend if possible. If you've been job hunting very long, you may be far more experienced at interviews than the person interviewing *you*! Take control if you can. **Prepare pro-active answers**, so you can proudly present all the information about you. When it's your turn for "show and tell," you must answer honestly, but you needn't elaborate on the unvarnished truth.

> *"Why did you leave your last job?"*
> *could be answered at least two ways:*

"I discovered that my previous company and I no longer shared the same vision for this industry." Or you could say: "That witch was on my case all the time and drove me up the wall. I had to get outta there!" **Which do you think is better?**

One of my friends was asked: **"Why should I hire you?"** After stating her professional credentials, she added, "I have never worked for any employer that has ever looked back and regretted hiring me."

If you are self-educated rather than degreed, you could say: "Since I didn't get to college, I became a voracious reader and I make it a point to keep up to date on everything in this field."

A little mystery is good! You needn't tell any interviewer all about your plans for your family nor need you discuss your love life or your age. If they ask, you can answer forthrightly if you choose to do so. If you'd rather not answer, then you need to appear open while you dodge the bullet.

> *If age is an issue, you can either*
> *confront the issue or dodge the bullet.*

EEK! I may be too young!

If you're young, I'm (Linda) inclined to encourage you to confront it, and re-frame it. Doing so indicates a certain maturity, which is exactly what you are trying to demonstrate.

> "I assume you're wondering if I'm old enough to do this job. I'm 23. But age isn't really the best criterion, is it? Aren't your *real* questions:
>
> 'Can she get the job done?'
>
> 'Can she work with the team?'
>
> 'Is she mature enough to stay focused on the job at hand?'
>
> Aren't those the real issues? Let me tell you about my background, education and work history...."

EEK! I may be too old!

If youth is not the challenge then I suggest, with all due respect, that you make sure your "look" is *very* current. Next, make sure your vocabulary is very current and make sure your outlook is up-to-date. Remember they have to think that you will fit in before they will even seriously consider you. My feeling is that people only come in three ages:
> "Young!"
> "Our age."
> "Old!"

The good news is that "our age" is very elastic. I have – and you probably do, too – very good friends both 20 years younger and 30 years older that I consider to be my contemporaries. And that is the aura that you are trying to create.

The really good news is that you may seem to be very "with it" because there is so much retro culture. (My kids think I am *so cool* because I know the words to lots of their favorite songs. So far they haven't figured out that I learned them the last time, and in some cases the first time, they were popular.)

You needn't be a teenager again, merely a contemporary of the interviewer.

Twenty-somethings and thirty-somethings seem to be far less hung up over age issues than their parents. My own perspective is that TV reruns have permitted them to experience social mores, life-styles and cultures that span over 50 years. Thus, they have a broader frame of social reference than any previous generation.

Find out what the twenty and thirty-somethings are reading and watching on TV if that is who is likely to be interviewing you. More and more that is the case, especially in technology fields. It is important that you understand *their* "punch lines" and frames of reference.

"That is sooooo cool!"
"As if!"
"Whatever."

Redirect the conversation when necessary (much as the youthful interviewee does) with: "Is that really the issue or would you like to know if I can get along with younger people who are in a supervisory position?"

They might say, "Tell me about your expertise in this field." You might say: "This is a field of work that I love and in the last seven years, *(never use any number larger than ten.)* I have learned it very well. I have investigated your company and I am convinced that I would be an asset to you because I can..."

If it's not personal but you need to skirt an issue or don't know the answer, try: "Without knowing all of the details of the situation, I'd be reluctant to draw premature conclusions." Analytical interviewers love that answer because *they* always want more information before stating an opinion, too. Show them the part of you that will fit in there if you want to get hired.

Power Tip: Rather than, "I *think*" which always sounds like your singular, unsupported opinion, try: ***I believe, I am convinced, My position on that is ... Historically ... Statistically ... Research indicates ... My experience has been*** ... Any of those have more power than, "I think."

> Our struggle today is not to have a female Einstein
> get appointed as an assistant professor.
> It is for a woman schlemiel to get
> as quickly promoted as a male schlemiel.
> Bella Abzug

Final Thoughts On Preparing For The Interview.

Keep the following things in mind:

🔑 Women are usually in a one-down position so you need to do everything possible to level the playing field.

🔑 Do your homework and plan to be confident and assertive if you really want this position.

🔑 *You* get to choose where you want to work!

> We are not interested in the possibilities of defeat;
> they do not exist.
> Queen Victoria of England

Linda Brakeall and Anna Wildermuth

Step 4
Make Your Outside Match Your Inside!

Here's a news flash for you: *Looks count.* No, you do not have to look like a movie star or a super model. But you do have to present yourself well enough on the outside so that they will listen to you long enough to get to know the person on the inside who can do the job.

Anna says: "Your image is content visible."

Linda says: "If you're smart and savvy, dress the part!"

Last year I (Linda) was hired to work with a client who taught for a national management association. My original assignment was to polish up her teaching and presenting skills because she was getting only average evaluations from most of her classes.

She was an expert in her field and she was sharp, but there was something wrong. After several days pondering the situation, it became apparent to me that her classes didn't appreciate her skills and knowledge because she *didn't look like an expert.*

With just a few simple changes such as a solid color suit, high contrast blouse, more definite makeup and a more current hair cut, her evaluations improved immediately. Then we added a little humor and a more definite, self-assured delivery and her evaluations improved even more dramatically.

Dwell in possibility.
Emily Dickinson

Step 5
The Actual Interview.

You must come across strong and confident walking in or you'll walk out quickly!

Inside each of us is a very high-powered microcomputer that analyzes information in a flash. People usually decide if they *want* to hire you in about 30 seconds. They spend the rest of the time validating that first impression and reinforcing their emotional decision with logic.

Make sure that initial 30 seconds sends the right signal. Be on time or perhaps a few minutes early so you can calmly gather your thoughts. *Be there!* By that I mean stay in the moment and focus on the conversation. Look pleasant, interested, and attentive at all times. Move quickly, confidently and decisively with your shoulders back. Make immediate eye contact, smile, and offer a firm handshake.

Initially, mirror the body language of the interviewer. You'll both get comfortable faster. After the initial "mirroring dance," keep your body language open and take up some space. Don't cross your legs and your arms and minimize your presence. Sit up straight and forward in your chair in order to look taller, project authority, show interest and demonstrate self-confidence.

Your hands are relaxed in your lap, or resting on the table, unless you are taking notes. Don't fiddle with *anything*! Not your notes, your nails or your pen. Eliminate nervous laughs and giggles. You are the best *you* that exists. They'd be lucky to get you.

As soon as you've shaken hands, start a friendly conversation and get the interviewer talking. With any interviewer of any age, look for anything that will give you a reason to start the conversation. Watch for clues as to his or her interests and things you share. Check for photos, trophies, and objet d'art. Look for common ground. "Oh, do you sail? I grew up on the Chesapeake Bay. I just love boats!" And then you are in the middle of a conversation, not an interview.

Find out about the interviewer, and figure out what's going on at that company and what they are looking for before you answer the *wrong* questions! A classic example:

> *A four-year-old asked his mommy*
> *to tell him about sex.*
> *She took a deep breath and*
> *went into the classic birds and bees stuff.*
> *The frustrated 4 year old said,*
> *"Mom, I want to know about 'sects!*
> *You know, like ants and spiders!"*

Really *listen*! You'll be able to give better answers. If you need clarification, ask for it *before* you answer. Listen to everything the interviewer says and ask intelligent, appropriate questions until you know enough to make a convincing case for hiring you.

If the interviewer starts asking *you* questions before you feel you know enough, you can appear open and cooperative while asking your own questions first by saying: "I'd be happy to tell you about that, but first may I ask you a question about... Just so I'm sure I understand the . . . (situation, etc.)." Ask your questions, knowing that you look great, you've done your homework and you are prepared for any questions that come up.

> **The test for whether or not you can hold a job**
> **should not be the arrangement of your chromosomes.**
> **Bella Abzug**

Step 6
Bottom Line On The Interview

Enter each interview with curiosity and an open mind.

Think to yourself: "I'm just here to get acquainted. I wonder what this person and this company are *really* like?"

Take a deep breath. Walk forward briskly. Shake hands with confidence, a firm grip and good eye contact and introduce yourself in a strong, firm confident voice, say "Hello, M-- Interviewer. I'm ____ ____. It's so nice to meet you."

One of my friends lost her job in June. She called friends to "Fix her up," went on lots of interviews and shortly received what she thought was a good offer. Within three days on the job, it became apparent that she had made a mistake. She took a little longer next time, and did more homework but that one didn't work out either.

By her third round of job hunting, she knew exactly what she wanted. More importantly, she knew exactly what she *didn't* want. At *that* interview, she asked tougher questions, she negotiated her compensation package better and — guess what? — she's still there. Maybe she could have found the right job the first time around, or maybe she just needed to "date" awhile in order to recognize a prince when he came along.

Finally, be yourself. That's who will go to work every day. It makes absolutely no sense to create an artificial alter ego for interviews. They'll either love you or they won't. *Someone* will. Hang in there!

Linda Brakeall and Anna Wildermuth

The rules for getting a job are just like the rules for dating.

🔑 You'll have to kiss a lot of frogs before you find your prince of a job!

🔑 Don't compromise your integrity just to get someone to like you.

🔑 And be prepared to go home alone!

Just for you . . .

List 3 new ways to think about an interview:

1.

2.

3.

What will you NOT do in order to have a successful interview?

What inspirations or insights did you get from this chapter?

What else do you need to know? We might be able to help.
Email us.   anna@personalimagesinc.com
            Linda@LindaBrakeall.com

Unlocking The Secrets of Successful Women in Business
Key 20

Keys To Verbal Power

As in many other things you have to fully understand the cost; both of gaining these new skills and of going without them. **What will it cost you if you don't learn how to speak and present better?**

As technology improves daily, it becomes obvious that specific information is often only a CD or Internet connection away. Information, knowledge, and details can be found relatively quickly. What cannot be found quickly is someone who can think, reason, draw astute deductive conclusions and present those conclusions clearly and persuasively. When you can do that, you will stand out.

> *You can often get close to the boardroom on your technical skills, but no one, other than the owner of the company, ever gets the very top position without extraordinary communication skills.*

The "soft skills" such as communicating clearly and presenting information in a user-friendly, persuasive manner have become marketable. At the top levels, if you can't do "stand-up," that is standing up and telling your point of view, persuading, convincing, and cajoling other people, you are quickly eliminated from the ultimate competition.

What does it take to gain these new skills? Mostly time. I (Linda) personally know of little that is wonderfully mastered overnight. It takes time because learning is incremental; you become skilled and competent one step at a time.

There Are Four Levels Of Competence.

First there is unconscious incompetence.
You don't know what you don't know.

Then there is conscious incompetence.
You know that there is something you don't know.

Conscious competence occurs when you take a class or read a book and try to apply the principles, concentrating diligently all the while. You know, *and you know you know,* but you have to remain vigilant to perform. After you have practiced, drilled and rehearsed for a while, you get a little less self-conscious.

The final level is called **unconscious competence.**
Every time you perform any action, be it golf, knitting, cooking or public speaking, you get just a little better and one day you do it well without thinking about it.

Remember when you first learned to ride a bike or drive a car? At first, it seemed like there was so much to remember all at once. You were self-conscious and you made mistakes, but you kept with it. One day, you found that you were not only *not* thinking about driving a car; you were putting on your makeup *while* driving a car. Not a good thing to *do*, but it illustrates the learning curve.

A dear friend, Jane Davenport, tells this story:

When I was 15, I prepared a speech for my Luther League (Lutheran Church Youth) group. When I got in front of them, my brain was frozen, and the only thing I could remember was the title of my presentation, and I said those words over and over and over again -- evidently hoping that the rest would come to me. It didn't. Today, in my seventies, I can still feel the agonized, embarrassment of that of that evening.

So I avoided speaking entirely for twenty years! Close to my 36th birthday, the American Pediatric Society offered me the chance to make a presentation to 587 doctors. I would have an opportunity to convince them that they should use informational films as a tool for patient education. I *had* to do it. How could I possibly pass up a chance like that? *I was selling informational films.*

I had to sit myself down and do some thinking. I recalled that at the age of 15, I'd had absolutely no knowledge about how to prepare or give a speech. Since I had written my own speech, it didn't occur to me that I didn't "know" it. I had read it over, silently, several times. I didn't know about practicing out loud. I couldn't have done that at home, anyway, because my brothers and sister would have heard me and made fun of me.

"Identify your fear and go there" is a quote that came to my attention as I was thinking about that big presentation for the American Pediatric Society. So I practiced and practiced and practiced. I gathered up my courage and I made the presentation. It was successful and my rewards for *identifying my fear and going there* were great.

Since then, I've done lots of speaking. I've developed, marketed and presented successful workshops for hundreds of people. I've been able to do all kinds of things that were fun and rewarding and all because I finally got to a point where I *had* to identify my fear of public speaking and go there. *Contributed by Jane Davenport, author, speaker.*

Many adults are still afraid of thunderstorms, or spiders, or the dark because of a scary situation that happened when they were very young. The same thing is true of speaking. Go back and revisit the "scene of the crime" when you first spoke in public. Relive it. Find out what frightened you and deal with it. As a competent adult, you can look at it with perspective.

Reassure that nervous teenager in you that now you have worthwhile things to say, hard-won knowledge to share, and a lifetime of experiences to draw upon. This time people will laugh *with* you, not *at* you!

You have to ask yourself:
"Am I going to let the fears of an inexperienced, self-conscious, hormone-influenced, uneducated teenager **who no longer exists** control my life?"

You have to tell yourself:
"I was young, dumb and self conscious then. Now I have so much knowledge to share! I have skills, talent and wisdom to offer in my own area of expertise. I will merely be telling my story to a bunch of people who came to listen to what I have to say.

This is the same story I would tell to a good friend and these are *just a bunch of good friends*. I can tell them my story. They want to hear it! In fact, it would be selfish of me to keep all of this good information, knowledge and wisdom to myself. I can do this! It will be easy and it will be fun!"

In seminars, I often ask who is afraid of public speaking and when they raise their hands to say yes, I say: "I don't think so! I heard you all talking on break so you are *not* afraid of speaking. You got here to this hotel today. So you are not afraid of being in public. Therefore, you are *not* afraid of public speaking. You know what you are afraid of? You are afraid of looking, sounding or feeling stupid." And once again the heads nod "Yes."

Isn't that a large part of it? It's not just standing up and talking. You can do that! It's being sure that you are well prepared to deliver a worthwhile message that others will find valuable.

The first time you actually have to stand up and speak to more than three people, you might fervently wish you could die. Silently you mutter,

> *"P l e a s e ! Just open up the earth and let me fall in."*
>
> *"My tummy feels funny. I might get sick. All those eyes are watching me. I probably look awful and I'll probably forget everything I ever knew about anything! Get me out of this mess and I'll never be a bad girl again as long as I live. I promise!"*

You do your first speech or presentation. **And you don't die.** You might wish you could, but *you don't die.* And the next time it gets infinitesimally easier. *Yes, that does mean a small amount.* And the time after that you'll find another microscopic improvement. Just like anything else the more often you do it, the easier and better it becomes, even if you are not making a concerted effort. Practice alone helps.

Besides actually standing up in front of people, mental practice is very helpful. Athletes do it all the time and the *trick is to speak often enough and well enough to find out what it feels like to do it well.* Then you can practice all alone in your mind and make remarkable progress. There are many stories of prisoners of war who mentally practiced their golf game or the guitar every day that they were imprisoned. They came home and played as if they had been playing every day because they had, *in their minds.*

What about that nervous tummy and those butterflies?

I firmly believe that it is not what happens to you that matters. It's how you internally *process* what happens that dictates whether you have a good experience or you are miserable. The butterflies are a fact of life for most of us. I know they are for me. Many other professional speakers tell me the same thing. The difference is how you *choose* to process those feelings. The folks who are afraid of public speaking feel those butterflies and think they are going to get sick. They think it's nerves. They think the butterflies are the internal panic buttons.

I like those butterflies! When I feel them, I believe they are an extra surge of adrenalin to get me ready to go up there and be my best. Butterflies are a variation on the fight or flight syndrome. I use them as an energy source and I *fly*! When you fight them, you are fighting *you.*

> ***Start telling yourself that when you feel those butterflies, it's a power surge and you are going to be <u>good</u>!***

Pro Tip: Take a really fast walk before you speak to balance your physical energy. It doesn't have to be long, maybe five minutes. If you're feeling droopy, it will energize you and if you are "hyper," it will calm you down a bit.

It helps to understand that the real purpose behind presenting and public speaking is merely to tell stories and share ideas. Your first thought might be that presenting better will help you professionally. And it will! But far more importantly...

Presenting better at your own staff meetings, to clients or to a huge roomful of people makes you feel close to invincible!

Just for you . . .

List 3 new things to say to yourself about speaking.

1.

2.

3.

What do you need to STOP doing in order to present with outward confidence?

What inspirations or insights did you get from this chapter?

Linda Brakeall and Anna Wildermuth

Key 21

Why Don't Salespeople, Job Seekers, Or Speakers Have Prepared Presentations?

When I (Linda) ask that question at seminars the top three answers are:

1. "I don't want to sound canned!"
2. "How can I prepare? Every client, interview, and speech is different."
3. "I just like to go with the flow."
   (My own personal favorite.)

Unlocking The Secrets of Successful Women in Business

Did you know that 67% of upper level executives write their speeches on the plane on the way to the meeting?

Doesn't *that* explain why we often fall asleep in the middle of their "state of the union" addresses? Unprepared is unprepared, but when you're the CEO, no one tells you how bad you are.

A few years ago, I was hired to coach the CEO of a major hospital in Chicago for his annual meeting. When we first met, he was charming, easy to talk to and "user-friendly." When he got in front of the mic, the charming man I met disappeared and was replaced by a robot that mechanically read his speech.

When he came off the stage, I said, "Can we talk privately?" "You know when I got here I met a charming man that impressed me." I waited a few seconds while he beamed, then continued, "Where did he go and *who was that* on the stage?"

He was not happy with me at that moment. In fact, it was touch and go for a while, but by "show time" he thanked me for my "honesty" and he delivered his best speech ever. It was apparent he was unaccustomed to hearing the bare, unvarnished truth, but ultimately he was glad that he did.

Unlike many CEO's, he was prepared with a script but he was not prepared to deliver the speech effectively. He didn't know how and he was afraid if he had professional coaching, *he would sound canned.* For the three years he had been CEO, he had woodenly read his annual speech as if it was his Saturday chore list.

> In matters of style, swim with the current.
> In matters of principle, stand like a rock.
> **Thomas Jefferson**

Linda Brakeall and Anna Wildermuth

1. "I Don't Want To Sound Canned!"

No one does! Our lives are filled with all kinds of situations where we usually say or do basically the same things every time that situation occurs, but we never think of them as prepared presentations.

Consider the art of telling a joke.

Before you tell a joke, you mentally check out who will be listening so that you can personalize it a bit. Many stories could just as easily be about three accountants as three attorneys, right? Then you run through the set-up of the story to make sure that you have all of the elements in place so that the punch line will be funny. Lastly, you make sure that you've got the punch line committed to memory, word for word, for greatest impact so they will laugh. And you have to remember to tell the punch line last. *That* is a prepared presentation.

How about dancing?

As adults, most of us have two or three little dance routines that we do most of the time. We vary them somewhat depending upon the music, the partner, the venue, and perhaps the quantity of adult beverages consumed. We do them a bit faster or slower, and we occasionally add a new flourish but basically it's pretty similar most of the time. That is another prepared presentation.

Or perhaps you cook.

(Apologies to Paula Poundstone, but Pop-Tarts don't count!) Most of us have about a half-dozen basic recipes that we manipulate according to what's in the fridge, who'll be joining us and how much time we have to cook. Don't look now but that, too, is another prepared presentation.

What do they all have in common?

They all have basic elements that have been committed to memory, that have been practiced often, and that flex according to the people involved, the time available and the situations. Most of our lives are prepared presentations that are adapted to fit the situation.

2. "How Can I Prepare? Every Client, Interview, And Speech, Is Different!"

Of course each one is different in the particulars, but they're all the same in greater scope of things. Everyone wants to know:

- 🔑 Will what you do benefit me?
- 🔑 Will you save me time and/or money?
- 🔑 When it's all over, will I be glad I worked with you?

People who resist creating a prepared presentation are afraid that they will lose their spontaneity when exactly the opposite is true. It's also a great cop-out. If you don't prepare and you are wonderful, you can say, *"Wow! Am I good or what?* I just walked in cold and nailed it." And if you mess up, you can say, "Well, I would have been better if I'd had time to get my act together."

> Behind every successful woman...
> is a substantial amount of coffee.
> Stephanie Piro

Linda Brakeall and Anna Wildermuth

Without A Prepared Presentation...

🔑 You tend to be overly concerned with what *you* will say next.

🔑 You tend to worry about leaving something out.

🔑 You really don't have the energy available to actively listen and respond to the customer, potential boss, or audience because you are treading water as fast as you can to keep from sinking into a missed opportunity.

Contrast that with the successful woman who has carefully researched her presentation. She has it well organized and illustrated with meaningful stories. She has back-up documentation at her fingertips. It is all arranged in a binder or on her computer so she just opens it up and all of her cues lead her effortlessly through her presentation.

That woman can relax and *listen* carefully for clues that will help her fine-tune her "pitch." She will be able to watch for body-language clues. She will be fully available, focusing *outward* on the client or interviewer, not self-concerned. What do you suppose that will do for her closing ratio? When you are selling, speaking, or interviewing you have two easy choices:

> **You can rehearse in advance,
> or you can rehearse in front of a client,
> an audience or a potential employer.
> Which is the better idea?**

Yes, it takes time to create a dynamic presentation and to indelibly imprint the elements that can flex according to the situation and the client or interviewer, but the alternative will ultimately cost you a lot more time, money and self-confidence.

3. "I Just Like To Go With The Flow."

Continue to do what you've always done and continue to get what you've always got. 'Nuff said.

> **If you want to increase your success rate,
> double your failure rate.**
> *Thomas Watson*

Presentation Basics

🔑 The purpose of every speech or presentation is to persuade or educate.

🔑 You must understand the goal of your speech. Exactly what are you trying to sell? A product, a service or an idea?

🔑 All presentations and speeches are simply based on telling a story. Tell your story with as much excitement, enthusiasm, and illustration as possible.

🔑 You must involve your client, customer or audience in your presentation or speech.

🔑 Ask questions and listen to the answers. In a speech, you'll have to supply the answers, too. You'd say to the audience, "You may think, (answer, wonder, feel etc.) that . . ." In a sales presentation, let them think about, touch, and try out your product or service.

🔑 You must ask for action. Get the order, arrange the next step, or inspire the audience to take action.

Linda Brakeall and Anna Wildermuth

You Say, "But I Really Don't <u>Want</u> To Prepare!"

Have you ever gone to work and left your brain at home?

It's happened to me more often than I care to talk about. Many times my extensive preparation and my repetitious rehearsal have saved the day. A well-prepared presentation will lead you point by point, reminding you when to tell stories, to ask questions, to identify needs, to sell the benefits, and to ask for the order. If you know it well enough, you can almost go on autopilot in that situation. *Not one's first choice, but some days...*

> ***Spontaneity requires a lot of thought and practice.***

A prepared presentation will avert disaster and prevent pathetically poor performance. More importantly, a prepared presentation will permit you to actively listen to your client/prospect/customer. You can focus on *their* needs because you will know that you are in control.

> We don't know who we are
> until we see what we can do.
> Martha Grimes

Unlocking The Secrets of Successful Women in Business

Just For You . . .

List 3 reasons for you to take the time the time and trouble to prepare your presentation in advance.

1.

2.

3.

What do you need to STOP doing in order to make better presentations?

What inspirations or insights did you get from this chapter?

What else do you need to know? We might be able to help.
Email us.   anna@personalimagesinc.com
             Linda@LindaBrakeall.com

> The other day my computer flashed a message:
> "You have been idle for a long time."
> Just what I need –   my computer telling me
> I'm fat and lazy!
> Hey, that's what families are for!
> **Anonymous**

Linda Brakeall and Anna Wildermuth

Key 22

Sales Presentation Homework

And *yes*, a speech and an interview are sales presentations!
(So is a first date, but that's another book!)

Many of these elements can be developed and used repeatedly in most of your presentations. The trick is to perfect the individual elements and mix and match as the situation requires. You will use the same concept for...

1. A general sales presentation, which will be used more than once such as selling computers, tractors or aspirin.

2. A specific presentation such as an annual company meeting, rolling out a new product, or award ceremony.

3. Any speech.

Your Homework:
    A. Gather information and resources.
    B. Clip, save and collect.
    C. Organize.

Step A.
Gather Information And Resources

These resources and information will help you tell stories that will persuade people to use or educate people about your product or service. Find things that will get them involved and lead them to take action.

Get yourself several spiral bound decks of index cards and several manila folders preferably with closed ends. This is where you are going to gather information. Yes, of course you can go directly to your computer and start the composition there but I (Linda) find that I often do my best thinking at times when I do not have a computer handy, such as while I'm driving, watching TV, in the middle of a meeting or in the middle of the night. I find the cards and manila folders give me a place to dump my brain.

Leave the cards on the spirals so they won't get lost. On each card you will write only one idea. You might want to get the index cards that have several colors on one spiral so that you can sort by topic as you create.

Techno-Smart Alternative To Index Cards
You can also collect your ideas in PowerPoint.
Write one idea per slide on the outline view
to collect information.

Start wherever you have something to say. Go back to the other things later. Don't worry about the order right now. When appropriate I've put in examples, and labeled features, benefits and closes in a side bar so you'll understand the components.

By the way, the list of things to gather
will look long and scary.

Don't let it bother you. Think of it as an inspiration-jogger. It is always better to have lots of information from which you can cull the pearls than to have too little. You won't have ideas or information about everything, but more is better.

In other chapters, you'll find details about how to tell stories, do a sales presentation (including closing techniques), nail an interview, and how to deliver a speech. For now, just keep track of your thoughts and resources.

Include on index cards:

1. All about you.

How you work, why you want to be selected to solve their problems, what you personally bring to the table, how you got into this field, why you stay in this line of work, your philosophy about what you do, your answers to their problems, your professional experience and perspective.

Jot down anything about your education and kudos. Mention college, specific technical training, certifications, offices you have held in professional associations, awards you have won, testimonials from clients, your strengths (forget the modesty!). And your weaknesses. **(Ex. 1)** Phrase this carefully. Be disarmingly honest and explain how you cover this weakness. Done

---

EXAMPLE 1:
"I've got to tell you that I am personally not very good at . . . so I've put all kinds of systems in place to back me up like . . ."

EXAMPLE 2:
FEATURE: "Collectively, at ABC Company, the five people on our sales team have 106 years of experience."

BENEFIT: "That means that you can count on working with savvy veterans who understand the problems that you have, and that if I'm not around you will have someone else available who can answer your questions immediately."

EXAMPLE 3:
FEATURE: "We don't have a huge sales team so most of the time you'll work only with me or one other person through the whole process.

BENEFIT: "That makes it easier on you, doesn't it?"

correctly, people will admire your honesty and it will build your credibility.

2. All about your company.

Why should a potential client/customer choose your company? What are your company's strengths? What is the experience level of company personnel? (**Ex. 2**) What are your company's carefully phrased weaknesses? (**Ex. 3**) Why do *you* choose to work at this company? If they buy you, they'll take the company, too. (**Ex. 4**) What is your company's carefully phrased position in the marketplace or industry? (**Ex. 5**)

3. All about your product.

Make a comprehensive list of features and benefits. List realistic expectations of performance and all product and service information.

EX. 4: FEATURE:
"Our company is small and efficient.

BENEFIT: "In this age of huge conglomerates, I find it comforting to have the same services and products as a huge company without the bureaucracy. I like working where I know all the people and I know how to get things done, don't you?"

EX. 5: FEATURE:
"We're not the biggest company in America, so we compensate by working harder than anyone else to get the job done for you!"

Remember Avis?
They made a place for themselves by claiming and defending the #2 spot!

Or . . .
FEATURE: "We're number one in the market-place and have been for the last six years.

BENEFIT: "That means that we have a great reputation to uphold and we want you to be so VERY happy with our service that you'll tell your friends. And that means that we'll bend over backwards to make sure we do the job right for you the first time!"

4. Objections and answers.

Pricing: If you're high-priced with quality, sell value. (**EX. 6. & 6A**) If you're low priced, sell economy.

Every other objection you've ever heard: After you've collected them all and typically, there are only about 10, write down the carefully thought out answers, too. Find appropriate quotes that help you deal with objections and your answers may come from other customers.

5. All about your client.

Collect observations about your business, product, or trends.

Jot down random thoughts about customers or clients. What do they want and need? What specific situations bring them to you?

Who usually buys from you? What are they trying to gain? Do your clients have anything in common? Personality? Behaviors? Learning styles? Quirks? Location? Industry?

6. All about the sales process.

Jot down sales process time lines; when to expect what in the sales process. How long does it take to get the job done, deliver

---

OBJECTIONS:

Example 6: "What will that cost?" might not really be an objection. It is very often a BUYING SIGNAL! If they had no intention of ever buying your product or service, they would have no interest in the price!

Your customer asks: "What will that cost?" A successful salesperson friend says, "You want to know what would all this cost? - pause- "If you buy it today or if you decide to wait?"

EXAMPLE 6A: "This answering machine is $380, but if you don't buy it today, it may cost you customers whose calls and business you'll miss!"(Lost time, missed opportunities, down time on machines or people.)

etc.? This is where you educate your prospect about realistic expectations.

7. All about the competition.

What are their strengths and weaknesses? How could you displace the competition?

8. Current situations that impact your industry or presentation.

What's going on in the world and/or local economy? Are there supply and demand issues? What is the impact of technology on your business?

9. Historical perspective on your product or your industry; past, current or future.

10. Statistics.

Gather all kinds of numbers about your company and the competition: Per capita sales, lifetime value of a customer, industry increases and decreases.

11. General information.

Ideas, thoughts, stories and anecdotes about situations, problems, resolutions that affect your business or product. Find dramatic or humorous illustrations, or drawings. Note places to add humor to your presentation and collect pertinent quotations.

> You may feel like dwelling on your limits or your fears.
> Don't do it!
> A perfect prescription for a squandered,
> unfulfilled life is to accommodate self-defeating feelings
> while undercutting your finest, most productive ones.
> Marsha Sinetar

Step B.
Clip, Save And Collect Things
In a manila folder

1. Save anything that might help you persuade, inform and educate.

Find things that will help you tell your story and get the client/customer involved. Collect pertinent articles from newspapers or trade magazines: Gossip and observations about your potential client or company, about your potential client's company's *customers* or your potential client's company's competition, or anything that impacts the target industry or its suppliers.

2. Printed information about the person or company you are presenting to, including their detailed annual report.

Clip out their ads. Find biographical information about their CEO, president and board members. Do Internet research on their company or industry trends. Check magazine and newspaper articles.

Check the 10K section of the annual report which will tell you what they worry about; such as liability and lawsuits!

3. Marketing tools.

Include all of your own corporate marketing pieces/ads, etc. and collect them from other similar companies for inspiration.

4. Miscellaneous:

Gather pertinent charts and graphs. Save cartoons, drawings, illustrations, and photos that illustrate points. Collect ads that work for you *from anywhere.* You may be able to adapt the ad or adapt the concept to make a point.

Save anything that amuses you or makes you think.

Don't worry about how or where you'll use it. If it is meaningful to you, it will find a place. Maybe not this time, but you *will* find a place. I have a wonderful ad! It's a color photograph of a big, brown, ugly warthog that is captioned: **"Just think, to a female warthog, this looks like Tom Cruise!"** I truly don't remember what that ad was selling, but it amused me and I keep it in my collection because I know that one day it will perfectly illustrate. ...*ummmm* ...something!

> If God had wanted us to think with our wombs,
> why did he give us a brain?
> Clare Booth Luce

> If you advance confidently in the direction of your dreams,
> and endeavor to live the life you have imagined,
> you will meet with a success unexpected in common hours.
> You will put something behind you
> and pass an invisible boundary.
> Henry David Thoreau

Linda Brakeall and Anna Wildermuth

Step C.
Organize

1. Sort index cards.
2. Organization methods.
   a) Mind map
   b) Outline
   c) PowerPoint Presentation *Auto Content Wizard*

1. Sort index cards.

After you have dumped your brain onto the cards (and/or *PowerPoint*) and into the folder, you have to find a way to make sense out of all this information. You have to find a way to tell your story.

> *In a sales presentation, the goal is to persuade, inform and educate with a sale in mind.*

You'll have lots of information on those index cards. Sort the cards into logical categories. Work with the three to five most important points in each category. Save the rest of the cards. They may come in handy later.

Using *PowerPoint* as an organizing device? Number the slides, print handouts, two or six per page, (depending upon how big you want the print) cut them into individual slides, sort the "slides" on a table, then rearrange in the slide sorter view. Make sure the slides are numbered in very large print (20 point), so you can sort them more easily.

The next step is getting your presentation in a logical, sequential format that *tells a story*. More importantly, a story that people will listen to because people love stories.

Arrange your material:

🔑 **Tell 'em what you're going to tell them:**
No more than three to five major points.

"Today, we're going to cover...."

🔑 **Tell 'em:**
Explain the details.

"We have superior widgets!"

🔑 **Tell 'em what you told them:**

Restate the three to five major points with different words and illustrations.

"So to summarize, we've discussed..."

> Perseverance is a great element of success.
> If you only knock long enough at the gate,
> you are sure to wake up somebody.
> Henry Wadsworth Longfellow

2. Organization methods.

Note: This is actually a better place to start than with the index cards, but most people (including me!) are uncomfortable with the required effort. If you can start here, and do the index card stuff afterwards, it will save you time and effort.

Use your index cards to help you with one of the following:

     a) Outline
     b) The Mind Map
     c) *PowerPoint* Presentation Auto Content Wizard

a. Outline

If you like outlines, you already know how to do that. Left-brainers love outlines. The content is the same as it is for mind mapping, (see below) but it is arranged vertically.

b. The Mind Map

If you are creative and right brained, consider mind mapping. Read <u>How To Think Like Leonardo DaVinci</u> for the best quick version of mind mapping that I've ever run across. (And wonderful thoughts on creativity!)

First get a very large piece of paper. (Easel paper or the back of a shopping bag will work in a pinch.) In the center draw a circle, and in that circle write the very specific goal of the presentation or speech. The goal might be to sell your product or service, or to establish a relationship, or to present the benefits of working with your company.

In order to accomplish your goal what else do you have to tell the prospect? (In a speech, you often need to fill in background information.) Sort through your index cards, write the most important three to five points in smaller circles surrounding the circle that has the goal in it, such as:

- The problem your product solves.
- The product.
- The company and you.
- Features and benefits.
- Pricing.

Next, what do you have to say about these items? Draw circles or radiant lines and insert the details. If you can draw quick pictures of ideas, like a light bulb for a bright idea, it works even better. A very simple version of a mind map looks something like this:

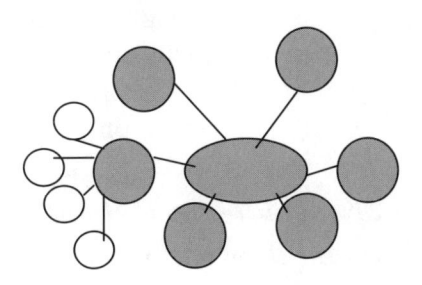

Check your index cards and folder again. Which stories will best illustrate your points? Which charts, graphs or visuals will enhance those points? Draw arrows to connect ideas. In what order would you like to present these items? Number your circles. Rearrange the whole thing till it works for you. And you are well on your way to organizing your presentation.

> We must believe in luck.
> How else can we explain the
> success of those we don't like?
> Jean Cocteau

c. PowerPoint Presentation Auto Content Wizard

You'll find the *Auto Content Wizard* in your MS *PowerPoint* directory under "Presentations." (**Toolbar:** File, New, Presentations, Auto Content Wizard Tab)

The *PowerPoint* Auto Content Wizard may come up automatically on your opening screen:

1. *PowerPoint*!
2. Create a new presentation using:
3. Auto Content Wizard plus other choices. Put the dot in the Auto Content Wizard and you're on your way!

"Auto Content" gives you topic outlines. Take a look at several. They are structured very logically. Some are specially designed for selling ideas. They give you a track to run on, especially if you are in a time crunch. You merely fill in pre-designed areas, answering questions and providing information.

The templates are seldom perfect but they certainly save time and they will get you started. And getting started is always the hardest part!

You can add, delete and combine slides as you go to customize your presentation and let it help you deliver a powerful message. Feel free to change the design and colors after you have created the content. (Toolbar: Format, Slide Color Scheme).

Pro Tip: Work in the outline section for creating content first, you can make it pretty later.

If you've never worked with *PowerPoint*, or a similar program, you'll be amazed at how easy it is to produce a thoroughly professional looking presentation. Studies have shown that people tend to think that speakers and presenters who come with prepared overheads, slides or a computer presentation are better organized than those who don't.

> **Master this software. It will give you the edge!
> We'll discuss details later.**

Just for you . . .

List 3 action steps to get your started on your next presentation.

1.

2.

3.

What inspirations or insights did you get from this chapter?

> The hardest years in life
> are those between ten and seventy.
> Helen Hayes (at 73)

> If society will not admit of woman's free development,
> then society must be remodeled.
> Elizabeth Blackwell

Linda Brakeall and Anna Wildermuth
Key 23

Preparing Your Sales Presentation

Overview: Five Part Preparation Synopsis

1. Good Questions

All sales presentations must ask questions to determine the buyer's wants and needs. Otherwise, you may try to sell them the wrong thing or in the wrong way. Know *whom* you are talking to and what they want and need before proceeding.

2. Good Benefits

All sales presentations must stress the benefits that the buyer will receive by buying and using *your* product or service. If they *want* the benefit, they'll *buy* the product.

Question: Why would you buy an electric drill?

Answer: **You want holes.** The multi-featured drill is the product. Nobody wants to own a drill, but ***you have to buy a drill to get the holes. THAT'S the benefit!***

3. Good Stories

All presentations must be illustrated with evocative stories that move your presentation forward. People remember and learn from stories much more than from raw data. That's why we love novels and seldom read the encyclopedia for recreation.

4. Choose The Appropriate Delivery Method

If a famous foreign world leader were coming to dinner, you'd carefully consider not only what to serve, but how to serve it effectively. You would also be sensitive to his or her cultural attitudes, and be sensitive to things or terms that might be misunderstood. You'd check out the protocol in advance so that he or she would be comfortable and enjoy the meal. Along the same lines, you need to choose the right presentation delivery method for each specific customer. The rules for presenting with overhead projectors, slides or computer projection are basic and easy to master, and they tell an audience or a client who's a pro and who's not.

You don't need a satellite hookup
or spotlights and dancing girls
to sell widgets in Peoria!
We'll discuss several options.

5. Good Editing

Don't let all of your hard work be ignored because of typos! Poofing, *excuse me,* proofing, by several people is a must!

Linda Brakeall and Anna Wildermuth

Your Sales Presentation:
Step 1   Good Questions

Begin a sales presentation with a list of questions.

Your goal is to build rapport, ascertain or verify their needs, discover their "pain," or the problem they need to solve, uncover objections in advance, and find their hot buttons so you will know what benefits to stress as you go along.

The best presentations are conversational in nature.

Use the chosen delivery method only as vehicle to keep you and the buyer on track and to ensure that nothing important is neglected. Conversationally asked questions also provide a little more getting-to-know-each-other time. (A section on questions follows.) Some questions can even overcome objections in advance.

A friend who sells health club memberships smiles and asks conversationally, during the warm-up period: "And I suppose *you are* the one who makes all the decisions about your own health, aren't you?" Most people say, "Yes." So it becomes very difficult later for the prospect to say: "Well, I've got to talk to my spouse before I make a decision." Got the idea?

Get permission to ask questions.

"Before we begin, may I ask you just a few questions to make sure we both share the same premises and I understand your needs? *I wouldn't want to waste your time telling you about something that wouldn't work for you.*"

Unlocking The Secrets of Successful Women in Business

This is not an inquisition!

Create a lot of questions from the following list but don't try to use all of them. Pick a few that seem to fit and use them as guidelines to create your own. Your questions must be pleasant, warm and conversational. If you sense irritation, move on.

Mr. / Ms. Customer, tell me about . . .

🔑 Your new... How did you choose that? (Phone, car, computer, furniture, landscaping.)

🔑 Your favorite salesperson.

🔑 The three best things about your current vendor.

🔑 Your worst buying experience.

🔑 The last time you had to find a new vendor.

🔑 Your needs, wants, concerns, thoughts.

🔑 What kinds of facts, things or information would help you make a decision?

🔑 Your company's buying cycle and how buying decisions are made.

More questions . . .

🔑 If you, M. Customer, were the spokesperson for your industry, what would you say to vendors like me?

🔑 M. Customer, if you owned a company that makes – whatever it is that *you* are selling – and could wave a magic wand, what changes would you make?

🔑 M. Customer, how do you use this product/service?

🔑 M. Customer, if you had a magic wand and could create one new product, technique or system that would dramatically improve your bottom line, what would it be?

When you ask the right questions at the beginning of the process, you can later tell the prospect, client or customer, about your product or service and tie it down with a benefit for *them*. Otherwise, they don't *care* what you've got. **(Ex. 7 and 8)** When you ask good questions, you'll be able to effectively tell your prospect the specific information that will interest them about you and the company. **(Ex. 9)**

When you weave your information into the body of your presentation it is much easier for the customer to absorb...

...and it sounds far more credible than when you stop the presentation to say: "Let me tell you who we are." That sounds "slick," like a pitch, like a classic "salesman." (Not PC, but who says, "slick sales*person*?") Your personal and corporate information has to sound conversational, like you'd discuss with a friend over breakfast, incidental to the story, not *the* story. Got it?

Example 7:
"You told me earlier that controlling costs is an important issue. Our wireless phone service offers flat fee pricing. That means you'll never be surprised at the end of the month!"

Example 8:
"If I understood you correctly earlier, a phone that has message display capabilities would save your salespeople some return phone calls. And time is what everyone is short of these days, isn't it?"

Example 9:
"Like you, we pride ourselves on stability. We've been doing this for 13 years and our clients tell us that..."

Yearn first to understand, then to be understood.
Beca Lewis Allen

Unlocking The Secrets of Successful Women in Business

Your Sales Presentation:
Step 2   Good Benefits.

Talk about how doing business with *you* benefits *them*. "I understand how precious your time is and I don't want you to spend any of it wondering where your order is. That's why I will fax or e-mail a status report to you every Monday afternoon. When you work with me, you'll never wonder, *What's going on?*"

Weave in information about you and the company as you go along. "You know, when Pat Chalmers founded this company 23 years ago, her one main concern was.... So she's made it a policy to . . ." This is especially effective if Pat Chalmers and your prospect share the same concern, then that information becomes a benefit!

What problems does your product or service solve? The usual benefits revolve around three things: saving time, money and making it more convenient.

"With our 'Just In Time' program, we can ship your widgets to you within 12 hours of receiving the order. That will save storage space and you'll have far less capital tied up in supplies. Wouldn't that make your life easier?"

Overcome obvious objections before they bring them up, and if possible turn them into benefits. "Many of our clients were initially concerned about our pricing, but when they discovered all the extra services we provide for this one inclusive price they found it was really a bargain!"

List as many objections and answers as you can. How many could you turn into benefits? You'll never use them all in any one presentation, but isn't it better to work with a full toolbox – just in case?

Linda Brakeall and Anna Wildermuth

Your Sales Presentation: Step 3   Good Stories!

Earlier, I told you to collect stories. Think back to the last time you heard a wonderful speaker. What do you remember? I always remember the stories. Stories, much more than facts, help you get that person-to-person connection. Stories make points and illustrate concepts. In a speech, stories are what they will remember long after they've forgotten everything else.

People like to hear stories about other people. That's why Newsweek's one page "People" morphed into an entire magazine. The only trick to telling memorable stories is to make sure that you spell out the point of the story. Tell 'em *why* you told 'em!

Let me tell you a story:

I once heard a famous speaker tell a long, funny story about unsuccessfully trying to feed his six-month-old daughter. He finished his story, looked at us all thoughtfully for a moment and went on to his next point. At lunch, I asked people what conclusions they had drawn from that story. And they were all different.

- One man said, "You can lead a baby to baby food, but you can't manage her to eat!"

- Another said, "Even the very young can decide what they will and will not do!"

- A puzzled third asked: "Why would he tell us a story about a baby?"

Every person at the table formed an opinion about the point, (or the lack of one) of the story. But no one knew for sure why that speaker told us that story. And I suspect that many of us lost his next point, trying to figure out *why* he told us about feeding the baby.

The reason I told you that story is this: S*pell it out!* Don't assume that they will "get it." They may very well "get" something else entirely different from what you intended. Yes, you may actually say: *"The reason I told you that story is..."* You have my permission.

Women often feel that we don't tell stories well.

Not true. We often don't tell *jokes* well. That is because many of us find jokes cold and pointless. But *stories!*

*A story that touches your heart,
that means something to you;
you could tell that kind of a story very well.*

So start collecting them now. As things happen, or you hear stories, jot them down on your spiral index cards.

Don't worry if initially each story is not a work of art. As you collect them, you'll find that often you can combine two or more to get yourself a rollicking good story.

As long as the concept is true, and you make a point that is worthy, don't be too concerned with being literally accurate. As the Irish father of one of my best speaker/writer friends, Rita Emmett, says when asked if his wonderful, rich stories are true, "They are all true. And some of them actually happened!"

Besides stories, similes and metaphors are good devices to pull the listener through a presentation or speech. "Like trees, we have to adapt as the environment changes."

Linda Brakeall and Anna Wildermuth

Your Sales Presentation:
Step 4   Appropriate Delivery Method

Note: The concepts and elements of a sales presentation, an interview and a speech are all very similar. You may want to skim this section even if you <u>never</u> have to do a formal speech or a sales presentation!

There are five – actually six – delivery methods.
- A. Flip binder
- B. Flip chart and easel
- C. Overheads
- D. Slides
- E. Computer/computer projection

The sixth, of course, is just "winging it." If you are closing 90% of your sales call with that method, then you just keep right on. In fact, close up this book and get back out there on the street. *Now*! You don't need me! *But for the rest of you...*

The best salespeople know their presentation material so well that they can merely glance at the presentation as they focus their attention on the buyer. If you are too concerned with what you have to remember to say, you are not paying enough attention to the buyer. You will miss subtle signals and that will cost you. That's why you need a thoroughly prepared, well-rehearsed presentation.

> If one cannot state a matter clearly enough so that
> even an intelligent twelve-year-old can understand it,
> one should remain within the cloistered walls
> of the university and laboratory
> until one gets a better grasp of one's subject matter.
> Margaret Mead

A. The Flip Binder

A flip binder is a three ring binder that has an extra piece attached that lets it stand up on a desk like an easel. Many salespeople use one to guide them and their clients through the presentation. It is a simple, compact, easy to carry and easy to update method that is appropriate for **very informal** presentations in low-tech industries for no more than three people.

How to assemble a flip binder

Collect appropriate marketing pieces, ads, charts, graphs, newspaper and trade paper clippings, cartoons, and testimonials. Arrange originals or excellent copies of information in clear sheet protectors with one idea per page. Consistent style and colors will create a "look."

You may also use your *PowerPoint* overheads in a flip binder. Use white or pale backgrounds with dark print. Insert a white sheet of paper behind each overhead in a sheet protector and they'll look quite presentable. If you'll never use these as *overheads*, then print directly onto paper.

How to use a flip binder

Position it on a desk, table or file cabinet, facing the prospect. "You know, if I stand right here, you'll be able to see everything and I'll be able to turn the pages as we go along. Is that OK?"

Statistically you will close more sales successfully if you can present standing up. The reason? When standing, you appear to have more authority, so your credibility is increased. Try to find a way to stay on your feet at least part of the time.

B. Flip Chart And Easel

The flip chart on an easel is sometimes used for sales presentations, but I discourage it. Unless you are a professional quality artist, a flip chart tends to look "home-made" and does not back up your professional demeanor.

Use a flip chart for v*ery*, *very* informal presentations. It is good for interaction with 1 - 20 people

How to organize a flip chart

Arrange presentation pages from back to front, so you end up with your conclusion on the front page, tidy and flat. Keep it neat by writing only on alternate pages to prevent show-through. Tape the two pages together so they are easy to turn, and provide numbered tabs so you'll always be able to find specific pages. Use wide tip pens in no more than three colors and **P R I N T** all words at least 2 inches tall.

Good use of a flip chart

It is very useful when you are soliciting input from a group. If you will have to write more than three or four items, ask someone else to do the writing for you so that you can concentrate on the audience. Easel-sized "post-it notes" will stick to walls and lined pads keep the notes neat. *When **you** are writing on a flip chart, stand to the side so they can see more of you than your derrière!*

*If you're going to get a lot of input,
have two or more scribes writing alternately
on several flip charts to keep the process lively.*

C. Overheads

Transparencies

Good for 10 - 200+ people with the right projector and screen. Overheads have been getting a bum rap for the past couple of years. "They're old fashioned." Well, maybe. But my overheads have never jammed up, crashed, eaten my presentation, or arbitrarily put something unexpected on the screen. The "techies" will tell you they have far less trouble with a laptop and projector. Much depends on how much you know about the equipment *when things go wrong*. If you have the knowledge to repair and troubleshoot, enjoy the high tech. If changing a blown out bulb is as high-tech as you get, overheads are safer!

I am aware that this is a contrarian point of view, and overheads certainly won't fly in high-tech industries, or in the boardroom. As in most cases, consider the audience, the message you are delivering, and *your comfort*, and then make an informed decision.

With a software program like PowerPoint for design, overheads are colorful, flexible and professional. I'm fond of them for programs that I present repeatedly.

There are some rules you must keep in mind to prepare overheads effectively. Overheads are not a script; they are more like the skeleton of an outline. My own personal rule is that my overhead should tell **me** enough to stay on track, and keep the audience/client focused on the task at hand. **They permit me to tell my complete story in a logical manner, to include all the important elements and they remind me to tell the right anecdotes, stories and illustrations at the right time.**

There should be enough information that the overhead will be perfectly clear if you know the information but appear vague if you do not. Example: "IRS" reminds me to tell a story about being audited but means little to anyone else. Those cues also give you flexibility. If the cue said "IRS story," the client/ audience would be expecting a story. With only "IRS," you can skip the story if you run short of time, and no one will miss it.

That's the information you need. Now look at how the two paragraphs of previous information would look on overheads. See the difference? It took two overheads and 26 words to give me enough cues to tell the complete story without cluttering up the visual.

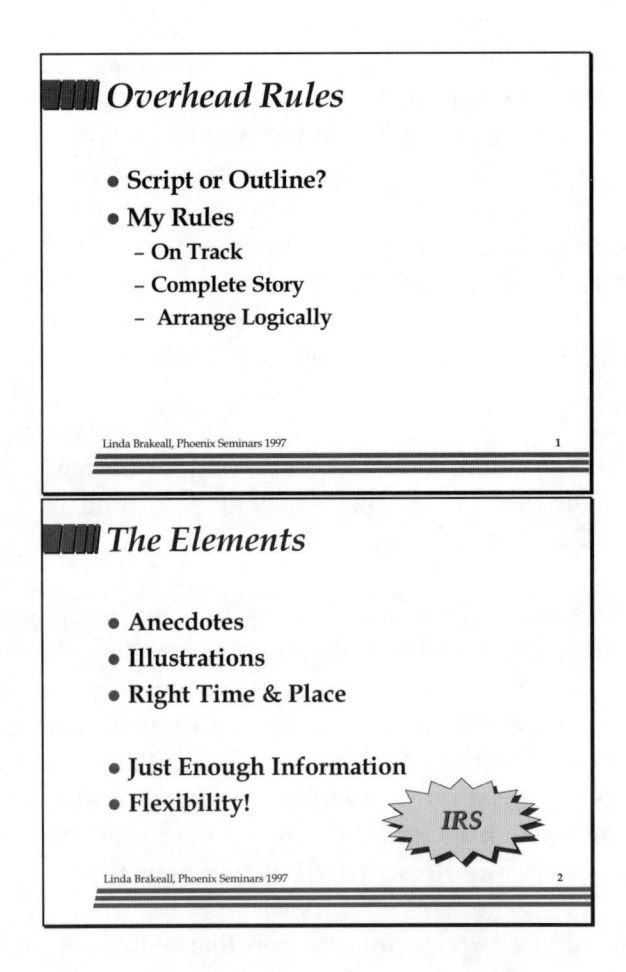

Overhead Rules

- Script or Outline?
- My Rules
    - On Track
    - Complete Story
    - Arrange Logically

Linda Brakeall, Phoenix Seminars 1997   1

The Elements

- Anecdotes
- Illustrations
- Right Time & Place

- Just Enough Information
- Flexibility!

IRS

Linda Brakeall, Phoenix Seminars 1997   2

Unlocking The Secrets of Successful Women in Business

Overhead Design Details
Use the same rules for computer and slide design.

Use pictures, charts or graphs in lieu of words whenever you can. A picture is worth *what?* Insert page numbers on the overhead master so each page will be numbered and should they get out of sequence, you can fix it in a flash. (**Toolbar**: View, Header And Footer, Slide Number. Check "Apply To All")

Use design templates to achieve a consistent look and use dark print with clear, pale or white backgrounds so the lights can be left on. Simple designs are better than cluttered ones and if you'll change the color scheme of standard templates, they'll look new and different even to people who use *PowerPoint* all the time. Colors will influence decision-making and how the "audience" perceives you. Red, white and blue is always a safe, powerful color choice. Pastels have no power.

Typically, no more than 7 words per line and 7 lines per page. Less is more! (I break that rule all the time, but it remains a good rule.) Eliminate most modifiers, stick with mostly nouns and verbs, and replace words with graphics when possible

Make sure the print is large enough and dark enough for everyone to read easily.
Most print should be bold because that actually makes the letters wider, darker and easier to read.
That means that all print on overheads must be:

No less than **18 point bold**

24 point bold is better

36 – 44 bold is best!

Linda Brakeall and Anna Wildermuth

Essentials of using an overhead projector:

Have the projector on a table large enough for the projector and your binder. If the projector has to be on a cart, get a small table to put beside the cart.

Place the screen across a corner rather than right behind you. They'll glance at the corner screen, but you'll get most of their attention.

Make yourself a last-minute overhead frame. Lay the first overhead on the projector and check the positioning on the screen before anyone else is in the room. Mark that spot at the top and at one side with masking tape. Layer more pieces of masking tape to form an **L**, so that you can slap the over-head into the **L** and your overhead will be positioned perfectly every time. You can also buy a frame - but they are hard to find.

Adjust focus knob on the projector or move the table or cart until the projected image is clear and large enough to be read throughout the room. Walk around the room and see if you can easily read the screen.

Practice putting your overheads on the projector and taking them off a few times until you are comfortable with the process. Have your first overhead in place before you start, so that you only have to turn on the machine.

Practice turning your projector on and off a few times, and find out where the spare bulb is stored and learn how to change the bulb, just in case.

Rearrange your supplies until it all feels right to you. You want to create a comfortable physical flow. That might mean that the overheads may go in the binder differently than you first thought. Or your binder needs to be placed on the ***other*** side of the projector. Use your supplies and walk around as if you are actually delivering your presentation until it feels right and you can easily — and gracefully — reach anything you need.

Never walk across the projected light. We don't want you looking like a hand puppet on the screen!

Look at the projector or computer screen for your cues, *not the screen.* Put one overhead/screen up and talk about the contents. Turn the projector off when you tell a story so that the focus is on you. It does not have to be turned off between transparencies if you're moving right along. You can also put a dark sheet of paper on the screen to hide the light without turning off the projector.

If you are working with a computer projector, use the B – B for black – key when you want the projector to look like it's "off." Press the same key again to resume. You won't risk a crash or have to wait for your computer to turn back on.

> ***Never use a chart or anything else that you have to preface with: "Now, I know that you can't read this . . ."***

If they can't read the screen, give them a handout. If you're discussing numbers on a spreadsheet, and it is essential to use the spreadsheet itself, make the numbers as large as possible – less than 24 pt is very hard to read. Use yellow fill to highlight only the pertinent numbers. Better choice: ONLY put those few numbers on an overhead or screen with a title such as: Projected 2004 Sales.

Linda Brakeall and Anna Wildermuth

Linda's Overhead System

Physically handling overhead transparencies:
One of the reasons people are reluctant to use overheads is that they remember watching someone else fumble with slippery pages separated by sheets of paper that fell all over the place. The presenter had to reassemble the pages in front of everyone and looked, shall we say ... *less than professional.* There is no reason for that to happen to you. People often come up to me to check out how I arrange my overheads, because my process is smooth, simple and practically goof-proof.

Print overheads on your color printer. (Read directions on the transparency film package so you print on the correct side, which feels rough. If you print on the smooth side, the ink will not adhere properly and it will run and smudge). Set them aside separately for a few minutes to dry. Remove the paper sensor-strip if necessary. After they've dried, stack with white paper between the overheads for 24 hours to set the ink and prevent fading. This is not required if you plan to use these overheads only once but it's essential if you plan to re-use the transparencies.

Put each overhead in a "crystal clear, archival quality" sheet protector. In a rush? After drying, put the paper on top of the transparencies *in* the sheet protector. Remove paper before presentation.

Arrange them in order in a three ring binder. They can't fall out. They can't get out of order. You can even insert tabbed index sheets if you have sections like pricing or delivery that you might need to refer to specifically. Put the transparency – *in the sheet protector* – on the projector, and *voilà!*

Handy tip:
You'll want a leave-behind in most sales or teaching situations. Most presentation software provides matching handouts

under printing options. Put your name, company, phone number, e-mail address and web site in the footer of all handouts.

A snazzy handout for potential clients can be made by printing the handouts in color, two slides per page, and having them trimmed and bound with a pretty cover at your office supply store. Finished, the little booklets are about 3" x 5" and permit your client to not only recall what you said but they can replicate your presentation with some accuracy to their boss, etc.

> **My philosophy of life is that doing your best at this moment puts you in the best place for the next moment.**
> **Oprah Winfrey**

Pro Trick
for classroom training or seminars:

I find a bar stool or a tall chair to be a wonderful prop. My natural pacing is *fast*. I often sit down to go over figures or tell a story.

> *Sitting down, or leaning on the back*
> *of a tall chair slows you down*
> *and seems more intimate and personal.*

I know this goes against conventional wisdom, but you might want to try it and see how it feels. There is no right or wrong answer. It's a matter of what will get you where you want to go.

> Don't go around saying the world owes you a living.
> The world owes you nothing. It was here first.
> Mark Twain.

Linda Brakeall and Anna Wildermuth

D. Using Slides
Use design and presentation rules for overheads.

Slides are good for large groups. You can easily incorporate photos and show the slides by remote control. You have some flexibility in advance because you can re-arrange, insert and delete slides.

My own personal reservation with slides is that you have to have a darkened room. Thus the slides are the show, not you. I'm sure that for the rollout of a new product, that is a good thing. For most sales presentations or educational situations, it is not. You might use slides for only a portion of your presentation that can *only* be effectively delivered with slides.

A photographer-speaker I saw recently used slides of his nature photographs in a darkened room because he was trying to lull the audience into a very relaxed state. It worked well. Is that the objective of *your* presentation? If you have to use slides in a darkened room, try to get a spotlight just for you, so that you are not a disembodied voice. If you use clear, pale or white backgrounds, you can leave the light *on*, even with slides.

**Vision without action is merely a dream.
Action without vision just passes the time.
Vision with action can change the world.
Joel Barker**

**If you can't be direct, why be?
Lily Tomlin**

E. Computer Presentations
Use overhead design and presentation rules.

Using your laptop for a one-on-one presentation is great because it gives you flexibility and looks professional if you are comfortable with the machine and the software. The really worthwhile part of using your laptop is that you can "stream in," "build," or "animate" one line at a time. (The terminology changes with the software.) If you are discussing the five major benefits of working with you and your company, you would stream in #1, discuss it, stream in #2, discuss it and so on. The new one is highlighted, the old ones are shaded but still there. Pretty neat feature.

Make sure your client can easily and clearly see the screen. Sounds entirely too obvious, doesn't it? But I've had people present to me and I couldn't see.

Tacky Tip #1:

In a one-on-one presentation, you will be sharing a screen with a client. Personal hygiene (i.e. deodorant, breath spray, easy on the cologne, etc.) is more important than usual and no garlic for lunch.

Tacky Tip #2: ...that *no one else will tell you*:

Talking a lot causes your mouth to dry out and a dry mouth causes bad breath. Keep a glass of water handy.

For groups, connect your laptop to a projector. With projection, and a remote control, you can use this method for any size group. Again, as with slides, the danger is that you will be in the dark, unless you use clear or very light backgrounds with dark print so you can leave the lights on. Get a spotlight for yourself if at all possible.

While animation, sound and literally all kinds of bells and whistles are available with computer projection, use restraint.

If you are working in a high-tech industry, you obviously will use more "glitz" than you would for low-tech industries. The rule is always: The stars of the show are your message and you, not the technology.

Take back-up.

High tech equals high risk.
Take the program on disk and take overheads. You can have the most sophisticated system in the world and a wire can short out, and/or the system will crash and eat your presentation. Or the projector you were promised does not materialize. Or the projector is there, but is not compatible with your system. In advance, plan for how you will handle alternative scenarios.

Recently, I was working with a partner and we had installed our presentation on his laptop. We got to the conference and the presentation had disappeared. Fortunately, I had it on disk and the day was saved. I could also have worked from the handouts, or dashed off to an office supply store to have had overheads made from the disk.

If you carry your presentation on disk also carry the *"PowerPoint Viewer"* so you can use another computer that does *not* have *PowerPoint* installed. The Viewer that comes with PowerPoint 2000 supports all PowerPoint 97 and PowerPoint 95 features. You can use it to view files created in both PowerPoint for Windows and PowerPoint for the Macintosh. You'll find it in the PFiles\MSOffice\Office\Xlators folder on the CD-ROM. If you installed the Viewer when you installed PowerPoint, the Viewer is located in the Program Files\Microsoft Office\Office\Xlators folder on your hard disk.

Your Sales Presentation:
Step 5   Good Editing

You often can't see the forest for the trees. You are too close to your own work. Let a disinterested third party edit all marketing and presentation materials for

Content	Style
Spelling *	Clarity
Grammar	Punctuation
Information Flow	Confusing Jargon

* **Spelling**: It must be read thoroughly several times by more than one person, to catch all the homonyms like "pear" when you meant "pair." Nor will "spell-check" find "hat" when you meant "what, or that or chat or fat." A typo I found in this manuscript almost got by me. I typed *making* for masking and spell-check didn't care! Fortunately, a proofreader caught it!

Proof red –   *edit*

Poof read –   *edit*

Proofread –   *Ah! Right at last!*

Ooops!

Proof read

Got it?

All that is necessary to break the spell of inertia
and frustration is this:
Act as if it were impossible to fail.
That is the talisman, the formula,
the command of right-about-face
which turns us from failure towards success.
Dorothea Brande

Linda Brakeall and Anna Wildermuth

Just for you . . .

List 3 ideas or techniques to remember for your next presentation.

1.

2.

3.

What do you need to STOP doing in order to be a more effective presenter?

What inspirations or insights did you get from this chapter?

What else do you need to know? We might be able to help. Email us.   anna@personalimagesinc.com
Linda@LindaBrakeall.com

**In each of us are places where we have never gone. Only by pressing the limits do you ever find them.
Dr. Joyce Brothers**

**We must become the change
we wish to see in the world.
Mahatma Gandhi**

Unlocking The Secrets of Successful Women in Business
Key 24

Landing The Sale!

Landing The Sale Is As Easy As 1, 2, 3!

1. How to ask for the order.
2. Silly but pertinent closing exercise.
3. Establish the next step.

1. How To Ask For The Order

After you've told them what they will gain by working with you and how you can solve their problems, don't leave the client until you have asked for the order. There are several ways to do that.

Adventure is worthwhile in itself.
Amelia Earhart

You can assume the order.

- 🗝 "Lets get this paperwork out of the way and you'll have your new widgets in less than a week."
- 🗝 "OK this paperwork and we'll get started!"
- 🗝 "Shall I send the invoice here to you or does it go to another office?"

You can ask for the order!

- 🗝 "Shall we get you one of these?"
- 🗝 "How many of these do you want?"
- 🗝 "With your permission, I'll just give the warehouse a quick call and see if I get those widgets for you in 24 hours. Would that solve your problem?"

Once you have asked one of these "closing" questions, be quiet and let the customer talk next.

Many a sale has been lost because the salesperson could not endure the quiet. Maybe, the customer just needs a few minutes to think. We often say in sales training that the first one to talk after a closing question gets to buy. If you don't want to buy back your own product or service, then *Shhhhh!* Be quiet and *let them* buy.

All-powerful presentations *ask for the order* or at least the next step in the process. (A speech ends with a call to action in order to influence thought and/or behavior.) If you have done your work thoroughly, you have found their real needs and wants and stressed the benefits to the clients as you've gone along. You've also created agreement and buy-in after you established that your product or service is indeed the best solution to your client's problems. If you've done all that, then the "close" is the logical conclusion to a series of events. **Just make sure to ask and don't wimp out.** You will not be perceived as "pushy" if you first establish the customer/client's wants and needs, and then offer solutions to his/her problems.

It's better to ask too often than not to ask at all! Think of it as opening the relationship, not closing the sale.

3. Silly But Pertinent Closing Exercise.

Rephrase the following bad examples into good questions that will advance the sales process.

Bad closing question: "You don't want to buy this, do you?"

Bad (really bad!) qualifying questions: "When will you have the bucks to buy my stuff?"

"Do you give a hoot about a product like this?"

*(Actually the original question had to do with a rodent's posterior, but in the interest of pretending that I possess some **wee** modicum of decorum, I (Linda) modified it for publication!)*

Bad question about the competition: "What's so hot about the vendors you use now?"

Bad question about the customer's business: " Why aren't you guys selling more stuff?"

Bottom line on those bad questions:

They are way better than no questions!
They are way better than no closes at all!
There are no answers provided, because
I know you can come up with something better!

Note: A well-respected and esteemed editor advised me to never use bad examples because, "Readers will do it!" I repeat: These very bad closes are better than none!

> Accept your genius and say what you think!
> Ralph Waldo Emerson

3. Establish The Next Step

If a sale will not happen today, then ask what to do next.

- "How would you like us to proceed from here?"
- "How and when would you like me to stay in touch?"
- "May I check back after _____ just to see how it's going with you?"
- "If we can't finalize this today, shall I touch base with you next week? Is Wednesday good for you?"

Just A Thought About Sales Presentations...

This may sound strange, but a short appointment or speech requires far more planning, organization and skill than a longer one. If one has all day, one can wander around the subject and will probably bump into the point of the presentation eventually.

Unlocking The Secrets of Successful Women in Business

If you only have 20 minutes, you must quickly:

1. Get acquainted, establish some common bond and get them to like and trust you.
2. Establish their wants and needs.
3. Tell them what you can do for them.
4. Explain the benefits of working with you.
5. Outline how you would proceed if they utilize your service or product.
6. Ask for the order. In a speech, you ask for action.

> **Though no one can go back and make a brand new start, anyone can start from now and make a brand new ending.**
> **Carl Bard**

Just for you . . .

List 3 action steps to land the sale.

1.

2.

3.

What do you need to STOP doing in order to land more sales?

What inspirations or insights did you get from this chapter?

Linda Brakeall and Anna Wildermuth

Key 25

Presenting To Big And Small Clients

1. Basic preparation.
2. Customize every presentation.
3. Customize your attire.
4. Customize your approach and attitude.

You can work well with a company as big and traditional as IBM and work equally well with a small, casual, start-up computer software company. Each requires a somewhat different approach. Typically, their culture and their style have far more importance than their annual volume or physical size. **Vary your style, attire and formality to match theirs. But never vary the thought, preparation, and logic.**

A Situation:

You have a presentation appointment on Monday with a big, formal company rather like IBM. Tuesday you'll give a presentation to an informal, average age under 35, Silicon Valley computer software company. They both have similar needs for your products and if you are successful, each company might give you a half million-dollar order. Six to ten people will be present at each presentation.

Step 1.
Your Basic Preparation

For a large company, you'll typically ask questions or do a needs-assessment in a separate meeting or by phone in advance. You will often do this with different people than the ones you'll work with at the presentation.

With a smaller company, you may be asked to do the needs assessment and the presentation all in one visit. Try to get as much information in advance as possible. You will probably get the advance information from the same person who will be at the presentation.

In either case, you must ask the right questions, get the right answers and find a way to give the customer what he or she wants in the manner he or she wants to receive it.

At any presentation, briefly verify your understanding of the information you gathered. The messenger may have given you the wrong message, or perhaps the situation has changed, or you misunderstood the situation. Try something like this: "I spent an hour with Bob last week and I've studied your annual report. May I take just a few moments to verify that I understand your situation correctly?" That tells the decision-makers that you've done your homework and clears up any potential misunderstandings before you plunge ahead in the wrong direction.

All glory comes from daring to begin.
E. Ware

Step 2.
Customize Every Presentation

Customizing will not take a great deal of time. Typically, a company like IBM will be more traditional. An informal software company will appreciate a little humor and enjoy artistic license. You'll customize less than 10% of any presentation, but it will make a wonderful impression. It says you know who they are and what they need. It will look like you spent a lot of extra time in advance and it demonstrates respect and caring for the client.

What needs to change in the presentation? Insert the potential client/customer company's name on the screens, overheads, or slides and handouts throughout the presentation, not just on the cover. Customize the benefits, stories and anecdotes for each company. You'll use different kinds of graphics. You'll probably use probably photos, charts and graphs for IBM, while cartoons may work for the software crowd.

> Any intelligent fool can make things bigger, more complex.
> It takes a touch of genius to move in the opposite directions.
> Albert Einstein

Step 3.
Customize Your Attire

For IBM you will wear the power suit, heels, and carry an expensive briefcase. For the Silicon Valley company, you'll probably wear slacks or Dockers with a blazer that could be removed, and loafers. You'll probably put your "stuff" in with your laptop, or in a tote bag.

Note: Never carry a briefcase *and* a purse. You'll look like a bag lady instead of an executive! In fact, why would you carry a purse at all in business? A small bag in your brief case for essentials will do. You want a crisp, uncluttered look and you'll be able to easily shake hands.

> Women have been trained to speak softly
> and carry a lipstick.
> Those days are over.
> Bella Abzug

Step 4.
Customize Approach And Attitude!

You'll do very much the same basic presentation for both but you will set it up and frame it differently. Be sure to maintain the tone that is appropriate for each client as you do the presentation you've so carefully constructed.

For IBM clones you'll convey a tone of organization, authority, and confidence. When meeting the decision-makers at IBM, you'll formally shake hands with each and address them by their last names unless otherwise advised.

When the spotlight is on you, you'll start with some variation of the following: "Thank you for your time. Let me give you an overview of what we're going to cover. First we'll confirm my situational analysis to make sure that I've understood your specific requirements, next I'll demonstrate some possible solutions to your problems, and then, together, we will decide how to proceed."

For the Silicon Valley company you can be more informal. The tone is laid-back, competent and *quick*. Shaking hands, waving, using first names and off the cuff remarks will probably work well. You'll set it up more like this: "Hi there! It's really great to be here! Love that statue in the lobby! You guys are doing some really cool stuff and I'd like to show you how the things that we've created could help you look even better, and maybe even get you home for dinner some nights!"

Presentations that are conducted as conversations, rather than "presentations" (she said in a deep, pretentious voice) are a co-operative venture; almost a duet, between you and the customer/client.

Check to make sure you thoroughly understand the situation and the needs as you go along. "Did I understand correctly that there is a time element we'll need to keep in mind?"

Ask for continuous input as you go along. "Tell me how could we modify this system to suit your requirements better?"

Validate the intelligence of the customer/ client whenever possible. "That's a very astute observation." (OK, so that's "sucking up." A little sucking up is not a bad thing!)

Agree with objections, align with the customer/client and steer them in the right direction. "You're entirely right! The process takes too long. This system traditionally *has* taken over 60 days for delivery. *Like you,* we knew that would no longer work. Our ordering system cuts lag-time by interfacing directly with our suppliers' computers. So we can verify that everything is ready for shipment before you OK the purchase order."

Ask yourself: How can I make the process easier and more user-friendly for those I do business with? How can I provide the specific services that are important to this individual and this company?

For a customer of any size, appeal to the <u>perceived</u> needs. Create the custom-designed package deal that will produce not only satisfaction but also delight . . . and referrals.

Unlocking The Secrets of Successful Women in Business

If time is the issue, stay on top of the order process, and give progress reports to the customer so it's apparent that you're on top of it. If quality is the hot button, have the order inspected twice before you let it out of your hands and be sure to tell the customer that you did that. If reassurance is what he or she needs, give them a better return/cancellation/warranty policy than anyone else is giving. And check in frequently to offer a little reassuring handholding.

> **You train people how to treat you
> by how you treat yourself.
> Martin Rutte**

Just for you . . .

List 3 action steps to make more sales.

1.

2.

3.

What do you need to STOP doing to sell more?

What inspirations or insights did you get from this chapter?

What else do you need to know? We might be able to help.
Email us.   anna@personalimagesinc.com
             Linda@LindaBrakeall.com

Linda Brakeall and Anna Wildermuth
Key 26

How To Deliver A Formal Speech

1. Speech dynamics.
2. How to read a speech.
3. Deliver your speech powerfully!
4. Microphones 101
5. Show time!

1. Speech Dynamics

The main difference between a sales presentation and a "speech" is in the delivery. You rarely have handouts or visual aids for a "formal" speech, so you must exercise extra care to be sure that you are clear and concise. You must use your charisma. You must be persuasive. You must tell a series of stories that lead to a call for action.

An audience tends to remember what you say at the beginning and at the end.

Unlocking The Secrets of Successful Women in Business

***Spend a lot of time on those.
Then if you wander a bit in the middle,
chances are it will not be a fatal flaw.***

I have a program that I usually start out by asking people to stand up on their chairs. Years later, someone will come up to me at a convention and say: "I was in one of your sessions when you made us all stand on our chairs." They don't always remember the specific program, but they remember standing on their chairs. They remember beginnings.

I often close programs with a poignant story about choosing how you want to live your life and people tell me in person or by e-mail that my story prompted them to take action in their lives. People have told me about changing goals, changing jobs, changing homes ...*and changing spouses*! They remember endings.

**Difficulties strengthen the mind,
as labor does the body.
Seneca, 3-65 A.D.**

**We women talk too much,
nevertheless, we only say half of what we know!
Lady Nancy Astor**

2. How To Read A Speech

Personally, I am not fond of speeches that are read, and I have actually only delivered one speech from a script in my entire life. However, I know there are times when that is the only option due to sensitive content, which dictates word for word accuracy, or time constraints when you don't have time to master the topic and speak with confidence without a script.

Here are a few speech-reading tricks that might come in handy:

First, have the print large enough to read easily so you won't have to bend over and squint. That might be 14 point bold or it might be larger. I like 16 point bold. Check it out in advance. Place the script on your desk and stand up to read it. It needs to be big enough that you can just glance down for a phrase and maintain eye contact with your audience. Next, have it printed in phrases, (phrase spacing) so that you will naturally breathe at the end of each line.

Example in 16 point bold:
**Good evening and thank you for being here.
We're here tonight to discuss the impact of
Pacific Rim companies on our stock prices.
As I'm sure you know,
they have become major players
in the past five years.**

Isn't that easier than looking at a paragraph that gives you no clue as to where to breathe? You can even highlight – by hand or computer – the main thought of each paragraph.

Five more speech-reading tricks, *mmmm* techniques:

🔑 **Keep your thumb on the line you are reading and just drag it down the page,** so that you can look up at your audience and when you look down again at the script, you'll know your place. To the audience it looks like you are just comfortably resting your hand on the lectern or podium.

🔑 **On the lectern, put the first two pages side by side, with page one on the left, and page two and the rest of the stack on the right**. As you finish reading page one, you glance to your right and start reading page two. Somewhere on page two, as you glance up at the audience, you will slide page two to the left. And so on. I know it sounds tricky, but try it with a stack of paper with numbered pages. You'll get it in no time!

🔑 **Dry mouth?** Try a Tic Tac. They are so small that most people can talk with one in the mouth. Keep water, a cough drop and a tissue close by too, just in case.

🔑 **If you will be working with a teleprompter,** make sure you get enough practice so that it appears that you are looking at the audience even if we both know that's not true. A good teleprompter-technician almost seems to read your mind. He or she slows down and speeds up with you. You lead. He or she follows. Again, "phrase spacing" is a tool to use to make sure that your speech goes as smoothly as possible.

🔑 **Breathe!** It's all too easy to race through a speech merely to get it over with. Relax! You are simply talking to people who really want to hear what you have to say. Breathe slowly between thoughts and let them listen.

> Winning may not be everything,
> but losing has little to recommend it.
> Dianne Feinstein

Linda Brakeall and Anna Wildermuth

3. Deliver Your Speech Powerfully

As I've said countless times before, (repetition reinforces learning.) being thoroughly prepared and practiced is the single best tool you have at your disposal to overcome nervousness.

My own personal preference for delivering speeches is to use the same format I use for my overheads.

- A well-developed, but sparsely worded, outline that guides me through the speech with cues to tell vignettes and examples at the right time.
- Powerful opening.
- Powerful ending.

Women tend to give the word "power" a negative connotation.

Repeat after me: "Power is a good thing." It is your use of power that makes the difference. In this case we are merely trying to find the power to get the job done.

Amateurs always ask me, "Is it really OK to use notes?"
I (Linda) can only speak for myself. Sometimes, I barely glance at my notes at all. Other times, I know that if I did not have them there, I would literally be "speechless!" I would rather have them handy, just in case.

Are there women who speak powerfully? Of course there are! But very few come immediately to mind. Isn't that a shame? Female politicians and business leaders obviously have to speak well in order to function effectively, but precious few names come immediately to mind. For now, the best suggestion I can give you is to watch the news interview shows on TV. Look for the in-depth pieces, not the sound bytes. You'll slowly gather ideas about what makes speakers powerful and what dilutes their message. Keep a list of who impressed you and why. How much of their power and credibility is based on their external image, the spoken message or the body language and "presence?" Is it the words, the person, or the delivery that says, "power?"

> When do you feel successful and fulfilled?
> It's not a day when you lounged around doing nothing.
> It's when you've had everything to do and you've done it!
> Margaret Thatcher

> We can do anything we want
> as long as we stick to it long enough.
> Helen Keller

Linda Brakeall and Anna Wildermuth

4. Microphones 101

Microphones come in hand held, lapel, lavaliere, with a cord or cordless. Stationary mics are attached to a lectern or podium.

If you are being invited to speak, you are usually asked if you have any audio/visual requirements. If you are creating the program or event, obviously you will have a choice. It's important that you understand your options. Using a mic well sends a message that you're a "pro."

In general, the sound quality is better with a stationary mic or a hand-held mic. If you like to hang onto something, the hand held is a good choice. Some of us talk extensively with our hands and move around a lot. We require a cordless lapel mic to function effectively.

All microphones are not created equal!

Some mics have to be close enough to almost touch your chin. Some will broadcast your breathing from across the table. The sound is adjusted by either turning the main unit's volume control or moving the mic closer or farther away from your mouth. My recommendation to you is to find a physically comfortable mic position for *you* and let them adjust the main volume. That doesn't always work but it's worth a shot!

The microphone sound test:

Get to the room where you are going to speak at least an hour before anyone gets there and ask if you can try the mic for a sound check. You have to try out a mic with someone at the back of the room to establish the volume needed from the main unit, how loud you need to talk to be effective: Will it pick up a whisper? What happens if you shout? You need to learn how to turn it on and off, and check for conflicting sounds from adjacent rooms.

When testing for volume, walk around as you would for the actual speech, and continue to talk or recite the alphabet as you walk. (I sing a Sousa march! Not *well*, you understand, but it works for a sound check.) Listen carefully for "hot spots." Hot spots are found close to microphone speakers, which may be in the ceiling, and they sometimes cause shrieks. Find them before the audience gets there and *mark them on the floor with masking tape* to remind yourself where *not* to stand. Have someone on stand-by when you begin to speak. Sometimes the volume needs to be adjusted again after the room fills.

Using a stationary lectern or podium mic:

Have the volume control and the mic position adjusted until you can speak into it comfortably without bending over. The lectern mic gives you the least freedom and limits your movement. However, if you're reading a speech, or need lots of notes, this may be the best choice.

> *Pssst! If you are scared, the lectern gives you something to hang on to and hide behind so no one will see your knees shaking.*

Using a hand held mic:

The usual rule is that a hand held mic should be about five inches (or one hand's width) from your mouth. That often means that when you hold the mic you can rest your elbow on your waist or your hip and your wrist on your breast, with the mic pointing towards your mouth and it will sound just fine. (I know that sounds tacky, but we're sisters!) Often the lectern mic is merely a hand-held mic in a holder or on a stand. In which case, you may remove it and have a wee bit more freedom.

Using a lapel mic:

Typically a lapel mic is fastened to your lapel about 3 - 5 inches from your mouth, about a hand's width. If you have no lapel, the mic may be clipped on a collar or elsewhere. Watch women news anchors for ideas on where they can be attached. Women usually need them closer to their mouths because higher voices don't project as well.

Test it and move the mic around till you achieve a clear sound that is loud enough to be heard throughout the room, without feedback, vibrations or shrieks. If you talk primarily in one direction, to the right or left, put the mic on that side. Be careful that your mic is not too close to jewelry because it will clank against your beautiful necklace or antique brooch and be disruptive.

Using a lavaliere mic:

The "lav" is a microphone about the size of the cap on a felt-tip marker. It is on a cord that hangs around your neck like a convention nametag. It is sometimes a challenge to pick up higher voices with a "lav." Be careful of necklaces and lapel pins that may bump into the mic and cause awful noises.

Also practice your gestures. If you occasionally touch your chest, you may bump into a lapel mic or a lavaliere, and make a not-too-attractive noise! Move the mic, move your jewelry or modify your gestures. I've always found it easier to move the mic or jewelry.

Unlocking The Secrets of Successful Women in Business

Final mic note. Don't be afraid of microphones! They seldom ever explode!

A microphone is a good friend and permits your audience to better enjoy what you say. Many people freeze up when they merely *see* a microphone. For those people, a cordless lapel mic may be a better choice, because once it's placed properly, you can ignore it.

I'm sure you've been at an event where you couldn't hear the speaker. Wasn't that irritating? Even more irritating than a bad speech? So be brave and learn to use one well.

You develop courage by acting courageously
whenever you feel like acting otherwise.
Brian Tracy

5. It's Show Time!

Write your own introduction in advance, which not only shows you in a good light, but also sets the stage for your speech. It concludes with: "Let's give a warm welcome to ......" I know it's hard to write your own introduction, but it's far better than getting a bad one, or not getting one at all. So write it and get some feedback from staff or friends. **Include all the things you personally would want to hear about a speaker, and the things that tell your audience why you are speaking to them today about this topic.**

What goes into the introduction? First tell the audience about the topic, then why *you* are speaking about it and any *pertinent* credentials you may have. Keep it short so they don't fall asleep before you begin to speak.

Print it in 14 –16 point print in phrases, give to your introducer in advance and bring another copy because it will often get lost.

You are introduced. The room rings with applause! You walk onto the stage. You have about 15 seconds to grab'em. Maybe 30. Certainly not a full minute. Assuming this is not a funeral oration, here is the best way to grab'em before you open your mouth. Be close to the stage or the front of the room. Walk quickly and briskly to the person who introduced you, smile and shake her hand warmly. Look around the room at the audience with a pleasant expression on your face, (about 3 seconds) and then scan the room a second time with the brightest smile you possess. (Another 3 seconds.) *Then* do your grabber opening that you have memorized. Yes, memorized! Really. Word for word.

Delivering the body of the speech. Unless you are reading a speech word for word, don't hide behind the lectern! Just by stepping out from behind the lectern, even just to the side of the lectern, while you hang on to it for support, people will perceive you as being more open and likeable.

Connect with that whole audience by establishing eye contact with just a few people in the audience. If there are more than 50 people, you can't personally connect with them all. But you can connect with several. Look for five or six friendly faces around the room and just talk to them. The rest will vicariously experience your genuine connection with a few people.

The 20% rule: 20% of an audience will love you because you remind them of their mother, sister or their first love. 20% will hate you for exactly the same reason!

As a novice speaker, one is inclined to "work" the 20% who seem unresponsive. You think, "If I can get *them* to like me, I can win over the rest!" *It doesn't work that way.* In less than a half-day, you are not likely to change anyone's mind. So work the ones who automatically love you. You'll know who they are by the smiles on their faces, and the warm eye contact. Tell *them* your story. Ask *them* questions. Listen to *them* laugh at your humor. They will actually help and encourage you. That will give you confidence and you'll be better. And the 60% who were undecided tend to go with the positive people. So 80% will end up thinking you're great.

In a sales presentation, you can elicit feedback and reassuring interaction as you go. Most people don't do that in formal speeches. If you can do that, you will be masterful.

Create interaction by asking questions. You can ask them to raise their hands occasionally in answer to a real question that needs a real answer, such as: "How many of you are in management? About half of you. OK, that helps me understand . . ." Done too often it becomes trite, tiresome and usually insulting. When done occasionally and appropriately, it is a wonderful device for connecting with the audience. They will feel you care about them and know who they are.

You can ask rhetorical questions such as, "Have you ever met someone who...?" Questions get them more involved. You can poll the audience by asking yes or no questions. You can ask individuals questions and let them answer as representatives of the audience. "Tell me, sir, how would you feel about...?"

You also create interaction when you move. When you move on a stage, walk with purpose or stand still. When you have a story to tell, or a point to make, choose a friendly face, walk in her direction and tell *her* that story, or at least a segment of it before you move again. No pacing! Stand very still to make a point. Move to talk *to someone.*

Move enough so that they are reassured that you are a living, breathing human being, but not so much that they are tempted to get out a squirt gun and see if they can hit the moving target! (Remember the ducks that went back and forth in the water at the carnival?)

Concentrate on delivering the message
to people who need to hear what you say.
Forget about yourself and have fun!
If you are enjoying yourself, your audience will too.

No pessimist ever discovered the secret of the stars,
or sailed to an uncharted land,
or opened a new doorway for the human spirit.
Helen Keller

Unlocking The Secrets of Successful Women in Business

Just for you . . .

List 3 new things you learned in this chapter.

1.

2.

3.

What will you STOP doing in order to be more effective?

What inspirations or insights did you get from this chapter?

What else do you need to know? We might be able to help.
Email us.   anna@personalimagesinc.com
             Linda@LindaBrakeall.com

**A leader is a person
you will follow to a place
you wouldn't go by yourself.
Joel Barker**

Linda Brakeall and Anna Wildermuth

Epigraph

Unlocking the Secrets of Successful Women in Business has been a labor of love for the two of us. We each hope that you have gathered some new tools to help you reach your goals.

From Anna:
My wish for every woman is that she finds the style that works for her and understand that it will evolve throughout her life. All of us have a style, and when you find what works for you, you will be brilliant and fearless in everything you do. Once you understand the guidelines and the consequences of not adhering to them, it is your decision to follow them or not.

Each of us creates our own self-esteem. It is based on the sum of many things; our role as businesswomen is only a part of it. As businesswomen, we are leaders, mentors, coaches, and team members. The way we walk into a room speaks volumes about our self-esteem.

In this book, we have tried to enable every woman to be the best she can be. We have given you the keys to visual style to help you showcase your unique personal image. As you build self-confidence, your interior self-image will be confirmed by your exterior image. We hope this book has helped you begin the journey of exploring your authentic style, and that your exterior image will help you be bullet proof even when your inner image is a bit tattered. "Your personal and professional style will promote and tell the world who you are."

From Linda:

I had been a professional speaker for several years before my husband had an opportunity to actually see and hear me in action. He was very quiet on the way home. Of course, I thought the worst. Finally, I got tired of waiting for him to say something and I blurted out: "Well, was I OK?"

He was quiet again and finally said, apologetically: "You really weren't any different than you are at home."

I merely said, "Oh."

He continued, almost musing aloud to himself, "It was like you were simply having a conversation. *With 500 people.*"

And I started to laugh. He was afraid he was hurting my feelings! But I felt then, and I feel today, that the *best* presentation of any kind is always "simply having a conversation" with people.

Linda Brakeall and Anna Wildermuth

My wish for you is that you become so comfortable with the powerful process of creating and delivering presentations and speeches that when we meet, as I hope we will, you can tell me about the conversation **you** had with 500 people!

We both send you love, joy and encouragement. You deserve it!

Anna and Linda

Unlocking The Secrets of Successful Women in Business
Resources for Further Information

Image

Title	Author
40 over 40	Brenda Kinsel
Body Language	Julius Fast
Body Language in the Work Place	Julius Fast
Business Casual Made Easy	Amiel/Michaels
Career Chic	Carol Ann Pierce
Dressing Smart	Pamela Redmond Satran
Dressing the Whole Person	Evann Maggione
Fabulous You	Toni Hartmann
Image Impact	Jacqueline Thompson
Image of Excellence	Grant-Sokolosky
Looking Terrific	Emily Chou
Plus Size	Suzan Nanfelt
Professional Image	Susan Bixler
Sex and Suits	Anne Hollander
Silent Messages	Albert Mehrabian
The New Professional Image	Susan Bixler
The Power of Style	Tapert/Edkiss
The Women's Dress for Success	John T. Malloy
What To Wear	Kimberly Bonnell
What's My Style?	Alyce Parsons
Your Executive Image	Victoria A. Seitz
Women of Color	Darlene Mathis

Color

Title	Author
A Rainbow in Your Eyes	Bernice Kentner
Beginners Guide to Your Color Psychology	Angela Wright
Dressing with Color	Jeanne Allen
Color Me A Season	Bernice Kentner
Color Me Beautiful	Carole Jackson
Color With Style	Donna Fugii
The Power of Color	Dr. Morton Walker

Make Up

Making Faces   Kevyn Aucion

Etiquette

Business Etiquette   Emily Post
Company Manners   Loise Wyse
Power Etiquette   Dana May Casperson
The Complete Idiot's to Business Etiquette   Mary Mitchell
The Complete Idiot's Guide to Etiquette   Mary Mitchell
The Etiquette Advantage in Business   Peggy and Peter Post
The New Manners For the 90's   Lettia Baldridge

Communication

Business Presentations   Tom Antion
Charisma   Tony Alessandra, Phd.
Choosing Powerful Words   Ronald H. Carpenter
Great Connections -   Baker/Waymon
   Small Talk & Networking For Business
How to Talk with Practically   Barbara Walters
   Anyone about Practically Anything
How to Win Friends and Influence People   Dale Carnegie
I Can See You Naked   Ron Hoff
I'd Rather Die Than Give A Speech   Michael L. Klepper
Talking 9 to 5   Deborah Tannen, PhD.
The Communication Coach   Cyndi Maxey
The Creative Communicator   Barbara Glanz
The Platinum Rule   Tony Alessandra, Phd.
You Just Don't Understand   Deborah Tannen, PhD.

Unlocking The Secrets of Successful Women in Business

Are you reading someone else's copy?
Get one for you or a friend!

Fax this form to **800-662-7249**.
Phone: **800-662-7248.** Have your credit card handy.
Email to: Orders@unlockingthesecrets.com
Mail with your check or credit card information to:
Unlocking the Secrets, 11 Arrow Wood, Suite 4B
Hawthorn Woods, IL 60047

Please send me _____ copies of
Unlocking the Secrets of Successful Women in Business
@ $24.95 each plus $1 each for S & H . (5 or more books? S & H is FREE!)

☐ Here's an extra dollar for the WINGS program!
☐ Send information on volume discounts for fund-raisers and corporate sales.
☐ Let me know when
   Unlocking The Secrets of Successful Men in Business is released!
☐ **Please send FREE information** on programs for in-house training, seminars, conferences, consulting, Visual & Verbal Skill Shops.

Name _____

Address _____

City, State, Zip _____

Telephone: (____) _____

Email: _____

Sales Tax: Illinois residents, please add $1.81 per book.
($27.76 with tax & S & H)

Payment: Check enclosed for $_____
Charge my Visa ____ Master Card ____

CC # _____

Exp. Date _____ Signature _____

Name on card: _____

FREE Success articles. Send email to Linda@LindaBrakeall.com.
FREE Image articles: Send email to: anna@personalimagesinc.com

329

Linda Brakeall and Anna Wildermuth

Are you reading someone else's copy?
Get one for you or a friend!

Fax this form to **800-662-7249**.
Phone: **800-662-7248**. Have your credit card handy.
Email to: Orders@unlockingthesecrets.com
Mail with your check or credit card information to:
　　　　Unlocking the Secrets, 11 Arrow Wood, Suite 4B
　　　　Hawthorn Woods, IL 60047

Please send me _____ **copies of**
<u>Unlocking the Secrets of Successful Women in Business</u>
@ $24.95 each plus $1 each for S & H . (5 or more books? S & H is FREE!)

- ☐ **Here's an extra dollar for the WINGS program!**
- ☐ **Send information on volume discounts for fund-raisers and corporate sales.**
- ☐ **Let me know when**
  <u>Unlocking The Secrets of Successful Men in Business</u> **is released!**
- ☐ **Please send FREE information** on programs for in-house training, seminars, conferences, consulting, Visual & Verbal Skill Shops.

Name _____

Address _____

City, State, Zip _____

Telephone: (____) _____

Email: _____

Sales Tax: Illinois residents, please add $1.81 per book.
　　　　　($27.76 with tax & S & H)

Payment: Check enclosed for $ _____
Charge my   Visa ____   Master Card ____

CC # _____

Exp. Date _____ Signature _____

Name on card: _____

FREE Success articles. Send email to Linda@LindaBrakeall.com.
FREE Image articles: Send email to: anna@personalimagesinc.com

Unlocking The Secrets of Successful Women in Business

**There comes that mysterious meeting in life
when someone acknowledges who we are
and what we can be,
igniting the circuits of our highest potential.
Rusty Berkus**

Linda Brakeall and Anna Wildermuth

Are you reading someone else's copy?

Get one for you or a friend!

Fax this form to **800-662-7249.**
Phone: **800-662-7248.** Have your credit card handy.
Email to: Orders@unlockingthesecrets.com
Mail with your check or credit card information to:
   Unlocking the Secrets, 11 Arrow Wood, Suite 4B
   Hawthorn Woods, IL 60047

Please send me _____ **copies of**
<u>Unlocking the Secrets of Successful Women in Business</u>
@ $24.95 each plus $1 each for S & H. (5 or more books? S & H is FREE!)

☐ Here's an extra dollar for the WINGS program!
☐ Send information on volume discounts for fund-raisers and corporate sales.
☐ Let me know when
   Unlocking The Secrets of Successful Men in Business is released!
☐ Please send FREE information on programs for in-house training, seminars, conferences, consulting, Visual & Verbal Skill Shops.

Name _____

Address _____

City, State, Zip _____

Telephone: (   ) _____

Email: _____

Sales Tax: Illinois residents, please add $1.81 per book.
   ($27.76 with tax & S & H)

Payment: Check enclosed for $ _____
Charge my   Visa ____   Master Card ____

CC # _____

Exp. Date _____ Signature _____

Name on card: _____

FREE Success articles. Send email to Linda@LindaBrakeall.com.
FREE Image articles: **Send email to: anna@personalimagesinc.com**

Unlocking The Secrets of Successful Women in Business

Quality is never an accident;
it is always the result of high intention,
sincere effort, intelligent direction
and skillful execution;
it represents the wise choice
of many alternatives.
Willa A. Foster

Linda Brakeall and Anna Wildermuth

Are you reading someone else's copy?

Get one for you or a friend!

Fax this form to **800-662-7249**.
Phone: **800-662-7248.** Have your credit card handy.
Email to: Orders@unlockingthesecrets.com
Mail with your check or credit card information to:
Unlocking the Secrets, 11 Arrow Wood, Suite 4B
Hawthorn Woods, IL 60047

Please send me _____ copies of
Unlocking the Secrets of Successful Women in Business
@ $24.95 each plus $1 each for S & H . (5 or more books? S & H is FREE!)

☐ **Here's an extra dollar for the WINGS program!**
☐ **Send information on volume discounts for fund-raisers and corporate sales.**
☐ **Let me know when**
   Unlocking The Secrets of Successful Men in Business is released!
☐ **Please send FREE information** on programs for in-house training, seminars, conferences, consulting, Visual & Verbal Skill Shops.

Name _____

Address _____

City, State, Zip _____

Telephone: (   ) _____

Email: _____

Sales Tax: Illinois residents, please add $1.81 per book.
($27.76 with tax & S & H)

Payment: Check enclosed for $_____
Charge my   Visa ____   Master Card ____

CC # _____

Exp. Date _____ Signature _____

Name on card: _____

FREE Success articles. Send email to Linda@LindaBrakeall.com.
FREE Image articles: **Send email to:** anna@personalimagesinc.com

> Others will underestimate us,
> for although we judge ourselves
> by what we feel capable of doing,
> others judge us only
> by what we have already done.
> Henry Wadsworth Longfellow

Linda Brakeall and Anna Wildermuth

Are you reading someone else's copy?

Get one for you or a friend!

<u>Fax</u> this form to **800-662-7249**.
<u>Phone</u>:   **800-662-7248**. Have your credit card handy.
<u>Email</u> to: Orders@unlockingthesecrets.com
<u>Mail</u> with your check or credit card information to:
            Unlocking the Secrets, 11 Arrow Wood, Suite 4B
            Hawthorn Woods, IL 60047

Please send me _____ copies of
<u>Unlocking the Secrets of Successful Women in Business</u>
@ $24.95 each plus $1 each for S & H. (5 or more books? S & H is FREE!)

- ☐ **Here's an extra dollar for the WINGS program!**
- ☐ **Send information on volume discounts for fund-raisers and corporate sales.**
- ☐ **Let me know when**
     <u>**Unlocking The Secrets of Successful Men in Business**</u> **is released!**
- ☐ **Please send FREE information** on programs for in-house training, seminars, conferences, consulting, Visual & Verbal Skill Shops.

Name _____

Address _____

City, State, Zip _____

Telephone: (   ) _____

Email: _____

Sales Tax: Illinois residents, please add $1.81 per book.
            ($27.76 with tax & S & H)

Payment: Check enclosed for $_____
Charge my   Visa ____   Master Card ____

CC # _____

Exp. Date _____   Signature _____

Name on card: _____

<u>FREE</u> Success articles. Send email to Linda@LindaBrakeall.com.
<u>FREE</u> Image articles: Send email to: anna@personalimagesinc.com